FINANCIAL MARKETS AND REGIONAL ECONOMIC DEVELOPMENT

To Christine

Financial Markets and Regional Economic Development

The Canadian Experience

SHEILA C. DOW

Department of Economics
University of Stirling

Avebury

Aldershot · Brookfield USA · Hong Kong · Singapore · Sydney

Published by

Avebury

Gower Publishing Company Limited
Gower House, Croft Road, Aldershot,
Hants. GU11 3HR, England.

Gower Publishing Company
Old Post Road
Brookfield, Vermont 05036
USA

British Library Cataloguing in Publication Data
Dow, Sheila C.
  Financial markets and regional economic development : the
  Canadian experience.
  1. Canada. Regional economic development
  I. Title
  330.971

  ISBN 0-566-07089-8

Printed in Great Britain by
Athenaeum Press Ltd, Newcastle upon Tyne.

Contents

List of tables

Preface and acknowledgements

This study is the outcome of many years of thought and observation, both at the theoretical and at the practical level, on the spatial functionings of financial systems. While I was working at the Bank of England in the early 1970s on IMF matters, it was beginning to be recognised by some in the field that the financial system affected developing countries differently from developed countries. Since then, the notion of differing burdens of balance of payments adjustment has become commonplace. Then, when I was working in the Finance Department of the Government of Manitoba it was apparent that the concerns of the Western provincial governments about the regional impact of the Canadian financial system raised questions directly parallel to those being raised in the international sphere. These provincial concerns have a long history, and still are given a high profile in discussions of the Canadian economy. The regional-international parallel is now particularly apposite, as Canadians express their concerns about the effects of the Canada-U.S. Free Trade Agreement.

My subsequent work on monetary theory and theories of regional development has suggested that there is a general argument to be expressed about the effects of different types of financial structure on patterns of economic development between regions and between nations. This was the basis of my doctoral dissertation for the University of Glasgow, with Canada as one of the regional case studies.

I was fortunate to be awarded a grant by the Houblon-Norman Fund to expand on this Canadian case study while on leave from the University of Stirling at the University of Toronto in 1983-83. I am grateful to the administrators of the Fund for giving me the opportunity to use my time in Toronto to travel around Canada, consulting libraries and discussing my ideas. I am also grateful to Erindale College of the University of Toronto for accommodating me during that year, and providing me with secretarial services. Gratitude is also due to the Foundation for Canadian Studies for a grant to finance a short research visit to Canada in 1984. Finally, I am indebted to Mrs Ann Cowie and Mrs Catherine McIntosh for all their help in typing and putting together the final manuscript.

Some material from chapter two has been used as the basis for an article published by *Studies in Political Economy* (Dow, 1987b) and a major portion of chapter three was published in the *British Journal of Canadian Studies* (Dow, 1987a). I am grateful to those two journals for their acquiescence in the publication of the relevant material here in book form.

My intellectual debts are many. I am particularly grateful (in chronological order of influence) to my colleagues working for the Government of Manitoba, to Professor Syed Ahmad at McMaster University, to Professor Tom Wilson, then at the University of Glasgow, to Professor Max Gaskin, then at the University of Aberdeen, to Professor Paul Phillips at the University of Manitoba and to Professor Ian Parker at the University of Toronto.

My greatest debt is due to my husband, Alistair. As an economic historian with a deep interest in Canadian economic history, Alistair had a profound influence on the historical dimension of this study. But, more generally, the entire study has emerged over the years bearing the imprint of our many discussions. This book is dedicated to our elder daughter, Christine, who already shares our fondness for Canada.

1 Introduction

Economic development does not proceed evenly among regions of Western economies. Can this fact be explained simply in terms of the different resource base of each region? Or is there a particular dynamic in regional economic relationships which imposes an uneven pattern of regional development, regardless of resource base?

These questions touch on complex issues. In particular economic development is a lengthy process, and uneven regional development inevitably means that some regions develop before others. This is most clearly the case (if we adopt conventional notions of economic development) with a country like Canada, where development has been associated with a sequential pattern of population settlement. How do we deal with different market valuations of resources over that long period of development? Is the financial wealth accumulated in the regions which developed first to be regarded as part of their resource base?

It is on the financial aspects of regional development that this study will focus. There is a wealth of literature which analyses regional development in real terms: in terms of factor endowments and movements, in terms of production patterns, in terms of market conditions. But the tendency is to treat the factor capital as being, synonymously, physical *and* financial capital. Here we will draw a distinction between physical and financial capital, and investigate what particular rôle financial capital, and the institutions surrounding it, play in the emerging pattern of regional development. This is not to suggest that financial matters are the sole cause of regional divergence, but rather to attempt to fill a gap in the current understanding of the regional development process.

The way in which such an exercise is to be conducted requires some explicit discussion. Within mainstream analysis, the recognised procedure is to specify a precise hypothesis and test it empirically. Alternatively, if there are two competing hypotheses, they should be specified in such a way that the data can discriminate conclusively between them. But, leaving aside the methodological problems with this procedure when applied to short-period analysis, it has severe shortcomings when applied to long-period analysis. Over the long period, the very changes in economic structure, institutions and behaviour which are the object of a study of economic development evade capture by formal mathematics or observation by consistent data series.

The political economy approach, on the other hand, forgoes precision in the narrow sense of amenability to mathematical expression, in the interests of depth and breadth of understanding of complex causal processes. The issues involved in choosing an approach to deal with a particular question are complex, and have been explored extensively elsewhere. (See Dow, 1985, Whynes, 1984, and Coddington, 1975, for example.) Suffice it to say here that an exercise in enhancing the understanding of a historical process, which has different manifestations in different times and places, is more fully dealt with by the political economy approach.

The choice of the political economy approach, then, governs the structure of what follows. The next chapter sets out the broad theoretical framework within which the rôle of financial considerations will be assessed in terms of their influence on the pattern of regional economic development. This framework yields the general hypothesis that financial variables do indeed play an active rôle in regional development. In order to understand this rôle more fully, however, it is helpful to trace a particular set of regional relationships; we take the Canadian experience as our case study.

2

The study takes on three dimensions in addition to the theoretical one of the second chapter: the historical, the empirical and the policy dimensions. Chapter three traces Canada's regional financial history, noting the contemporary perceptions within each region of how financial variables impinged on the regional economy. Reference is made to some case studies of particular localities in particular periods. These provide the most informative 'tests' of the general hypothesis developed in chapter two. In chapter four, however, we explore the possibility of more conventional tests, using aggregative data which are comparable across regions. In the process, we go through the exercise of setting out precisely what aggregative regional financial data are in fact available for Canada, in order to assess the feasibility of conventional hypothesis-testing. The data are presented in such a way as to allow some assessment of the general hypothesis proposed here, and the methodological issues involved in this task are discussed. Finally, economic theory serves not only to promote understanding, but also to assist in dealing with policy issues. Chapter five explores the various policy questions to which the foregoing analysis can contribute, and suggests some conclusions.

Canada provides a particularly interesting case study. As with most countries, the pattern of regional economic development has been a major force in Canada's economic and political history. But the rôle of national and regional financial institutions has been a recurring issue in debates over the distribution of economic and political power. The issue has thus been subject to scrutiny at both the political and academic levels, it has prompted financial institutions to publish regional data and it has encouraged provincial governments to initiate actions designed to modify financial behaviour as it affects the provincial economies.

The same could be said of the United States, where there is a more well-developed academic literature on the subject. But the two cases differ in a fundamental respect. The Canadian financial system is, essentially, a national one, with nationwide branching of most major financial institutions (particularly at the retail end of the financial system). The United States, in contrast, has traditionally had a regionally-segmented financial system, to the extent of a regionalised monetary authority and state restrictions on bank branching (although this latter feature is now breaking down). This difference

3

is fundamental in the case of the argument, frequently expressed, that the more integrated the national financial system, the more it contributes to regional economic convergence.

Canada's regional disparities are not as severe as in some Western countries, but they are nevertheless significant. Taking the conventional (albeit limited) measure of per capita income as an indicator of relative development, the average in the Atlantic region was still only two-thirds of the Ontario average in 1980. While Prairie incomes (primarily in Alberta) rose above the national average in the late 1970s and early 1980s on the basis of natural resource revenues, subsequent reversals in the oil and gas industries have started a sharp downswing in the unstable cyclical pattern typical of this natural resource-dependent region.

In the terminology of dependency theory, the Golden Horseshoe area of Ontario, plus Montreal, most closely resembles the Metropolis, with their concentration on manufacturing amd service industries. Most of the rest of Canada resembles the Hinterland in being heavily dependent on primary products and related industries. The Atlantic economy is dependent on forest products, coal and steel, and fishing, most of Quebec on agriculture and low-technology industry, Northern Ontario on forest products and mining, the Prairies on agriculture, mining and oil and gas, and British Columbia (BC) on forest products and mining. The persistence of this economic structure over a century can be explained to a considerable extent by the trading arrangements arising from the National Policy of 1879 (implemented in some form until the 1930s) which was designed to protect and promote Central Canadian manufacturing industry, and by the pattern of investment arising from the concentration of wealth and of financial institutions in that area.

Dependency theory focuses on the formative influence, on economic structure and development, of the trade and investment conditions facing an economy. This body of theory will influence the theoretical approach set out in the next chapter. For a monetary dimension to the analysis, dependency theory will be combined with Post Keynesian monetary theory. Post Keynesian theory, unlike mainstream theory, posits an influence of monetary variables on output and employment in both the short-period and the long-period. It is useful to discuss the relevance of this approach to regional

4

economies. But we begin by discussing the current state of theory as it pertains to regional disparities, and the rôle of financial variables therein.

Finally, while we start the next chapter with a brief review of the literature on finance and regional development in general, it is worthwhile at this point to specify the particular contribution intended with this study. Much of the material is drawn from secondary sources, and many of the ideas have been expressed elsewhere. The purpose here is to draw together disparate sets of material within a coherent framework: monetary theory with Canadian economic history, policy issues with a thorough explanation of the available data (in contrast to the customary assertions as to their paucity). It is the creative admixture of facts and ideas from different subdisciplines which is the hallmark of political economy. In particular, there has been no complete study of the issue as it applies to Canada, nor indeed any with the particular theoretical perspective adopted here. While any conclusion over the importance of monetary variables for regional development must rely crucially on the micro case-study evidence, it is important to put these case studies into a broad, macroeconomic perspective.

2 A theory of finance and regional development

2.1. INTRODUCTION

Underlying any perceptions of the regional development process is a particular understanding of how capitalist economies function, and how best they should be analysed. Thus the general tenor of theories of regional development is taken from the schools of thought to which their expositors subscribe. We start, therefore, with a brief general discussion of the ways in which regional development has been analysed in the past, to set the scene for our discussion of financial variables.

The orthodox mainstream theory is set in a general equilibrium framework. Full general equilibrium requires factor price equalisation and full employment of factors. Thus, in equilibrium, incomes may only differ between regions as a result of differing factor endowments (e.g. a higher skill level in the labor force) and no unemployment can persist. Mainstream theories thus focus on the adjustment mechanisms by which regional equilibrium, once disturbed, is restored. (See Holland 1976, chapter 1 for a review.) The implication that there is little to be said about persistent differences in regional incomes and unemployment rates has not prevented the identification of this approach, by many, with regional economics. This perhaps only less at odds with the issue of uneven development than u... equivalent theoretical approach to international economics, which likewise examines the conditions for factor price equalisation. (Indeed the mainstream regional and international theories were originally developed in parallel by Ohlin 1933.)

However, the Canadian mainstream literature on regional development has thrown up an interesting theory, called the transfer dependency theory, which does explain persistent uneven regional development: as an equilibrium, rather than a disequilibrium phenomenon. This theory, first introduced by Courchene (1978, 1981, 1986) and now gaining widespread support, suggests that fiscal transfers to high unemployment/low income regions create a dependency equilibrium. The normal market incentives for factor flows to equalise factor prices are offset by transfer payments. As a corollary, the cure for uneven development is the elimination of transfer payments.

The Macdonald Commission, whose report (Government of Canada 1986) lent support to the transfer dependency theory, at the same time was supported by a range of research reports which contain surveys of the Canadian literature on regional development (Mansell and Copithorne 1986 and Vanderkamp 1986). Both surveys conclude that transfer dependency plays a part in the pattern of regional development in Canada, along with such factors as regional differences in preferences, and in costs of factor and goods mobility. The consensus of the mainstream literature, therefore, is that uneven regional development is the result of a combination of impediments to attaining equilibrium on the one hand, and the character of that equilibrium on the other. The policy implications for Canada of this consensus will be discussed in more detail in chapter five.

Orthodox Marxian theory has had little to contribute to explanations of uneven regional development, although Marx did discuss particular regional questions and posited an antagonism between country and city. But spatial divisions cut across class divisions. So there has been a strong resistance among orthodox Marxists to probing regional questions for fear of fostering divisions within the working class. However, a variety of theories has been developed in an attempt to provide a Marxian view of regional development;

7

examples are applications of Lenin's (1916) theory of imperialism to regions, and Mandel's (1973) theory of the regional disposition of the reserve army of the unemployed. But Edel *et al.* (1978) punctuate an excellent review of the radical regional literature with the observation that none of these theories provides a satisfactorily class-based analysis.

Nevertheless, as long as one is prepared to countenance theories not explicitly grounded in class analysis, there is a wide range of useful theories in the middle ground between orthodox mainstream and orthodox Marxian analysis. Of these, the two we will concentrate on here are the theory of cumulative causation, originated by Myrdal (1964) and adopted by Keynesians (notably Kaldor 1970, and Thirlwall 1980, 1986), and dependency theory originated by neo-Marxians such as Frank (1966), Baran (1957), Cardoso and Falletto (1969), Amin (1974) and Wallerstein (1976). In the Canadian literature, see Vanderkamp (1986) for an account of cumulation causation theory, particularly as manifested in labour market behaviour, and Matthews (1983, pp.57-68) for an account of dependency theory in relation to transfer dependency theory. Both bodies of theory explain uneven regional development systematically, as an inherent feature of capitalist economies; the slow growth of some regions is a consequence of the faster growth of others. Both differ from most neo-classical theory by considering systematic regional differences in returns to factors.

Cumulative causation theory stresses the competitive advantages enjoyed by those regions already most developed; growth itself allows dynamic economies of scale to be reaped in a variety of contexts, leading to faster productivity growth, which makes it even harder for other regions to compete. These negative, 'backwash', effects are nevertheless offset by positive, 'spread' effects: the adoption of new technology by backward regions, an expanding market for their products in the faster-growing regions, and so on. (Myrdal, 1964, in fact argued that spread effects tend to dominate backwash effects among regions, though not among nations.)

Among the sectors of central regions which enjoy dynamic economies of scale, according to cumulative causation theory, is the financial sector. The fact that financial institutions will tend to have head offices in the central regions implies a remoteness from sources of investment finance for

8

businesses in peripheral regions; these businesses experience difficulties in borrowing in the same way as, in general, small businesses experience more difficulties than large businesses (because of the smaller size of loans relative to fixed processing costs, lack of information, etc.).

Dependency theory similarly focuses on systematic regional differences in marginal efficiency of capital, but emphasises more than cumulative causation theory the dependence of peripheral regions on natural resource production and of central regions on manufacturing. Differences in returns to investment are thus explained in relation to different production patterns; underlying these patterns is the power relationship they entail. Returns on primary production are highly variable, determined by patterns of demand set in the centre. The dependent pattern of trade and investment follows from the different characteristics of primary and secondary production.

As a corollary, since historically wealth resides in the centre, peripheral regions are dependent on capital inflows to finance investment. These flows are erratic, in line with the erratic pattern of returns on primary production, exacerbating the dependency relationship. But, while Lenin had explored the portfolio investment aspects of the dependency relationship, the modern literature focuses on direct investment. Even then, Lenin's interest was in the distribution of a given surplus between finance and other capitalists. Significant though the distribution of surplus and the pattern of direct investment are, the neglect of concern with the monetary aspects of financial flows has left untouched an important facet of dependency.

Cumulative causation theory and dependency theory combine well for application to a study of the Canadian regions. The former explains why disparities in returns emerge in any given area of production, leading to disparities in wealth which can then reinforce any tendency for regional specialisation in primary or secondary production. Dependency theory explains the difficulties experienced by peripheral economies arising from concentration on primary production. The power relationship aspect of dependency theory, combined with cumulative causation theory further explains the difficulties involved in promoting a more balanced regional pattern of production.

But not much has been made of the financial aspects of either theory.

9

Indeed Keynesians like Kaldor who have developed cumulative causation theory in the regional context are noted for their view that the supply of money is endogenous at the national and regional levels; banks are prepared to supply advances indefinitely at a set interest rate, and acquire the reserves required to back the increase in deposits after the fact. In other words, all potential borrowers face the same borrowing conditions; all the emphasis is put on their expectations as to the return on their investment (relative to the going interest rate) since these determine investment plans. Money plays no active rôle in investment decisions, and thus in promoting uneven development.

Mainstream theorists go further, arguing that national financial markets if anything make regional development *more* even. Financial flows between regions are in fact a key variable in adjustment to equilibrium. Disequilibrium may be the result of an inequality of savings and investment in each region. If exports from one region are low relative to imports, there will be insufficient saving to finance investment; but the resulting excess demand for funds will be met by an inflow of funds from the other regions with high exports and thus excess saving, according to Scitovsky (1957). This process ensures equalisation of returns on physical and financial capital. If capital is earning a low return in one region relative to others, the outflow of capital will raise the average return on remaining projects in that region and lower it in others, promoting equality (according to Mundell 1976). This adjustment process for the Canadian regions is expressed explicitly in terms of the price-specie-flow mechanism of the gold standard system by Courchene (1978, 1986).

But in addition to ease of interregional capital mobility there is what Ingram (1959) calls the stock of 'generalised claims', i.e. financial instruments such as government bonds which are traded nationally. Any temporary fluctuation in expected earnings or in purchases of regional securities need not have the multiple effect on regional bank lending which would be suggested by bank multiplier theory. Faced with a reduction in deposits, banks can maintain their reserves by selling generalised claims rather than by calling in advances.

The problem of course, as Pfister (1960) and Whitman (1967) have argued, is that regional differences in export performance and ability to attract capital are not generally temporary. Low export growth tends to mean poor investment prospects regardless of how much saving is available and is thus more likely to encourage continued outflows of funds than inflows. By the time this process raises the return on the remaining capital to that of capital in other regions, there may be very little economic activity left.

In mainstream theory, then, financial and physical capital are equivalent since investment finance is equated with saving; regions benefit from having extra-regional outlets for saving (when the local return on investment is low) or sources of additional saving (when the local return on investment is high). Financial institutions intermediate between savers and investors. Even more importance is placed on planned regional investment by cumulative causation theorists, because planned saving is not regarded as a constraint; financial institutions create money to finance investment, which generates income and thereby the saving to fund the investment finance. For both sets of theory, therefore, regional financial conditions are unimportant; it is the national cost of borrowing saving, in the mainstream case, and the interest rate determined by the national monetary authorities, in the cumulative causation case, which constitute the financial input to the regional investment decision.

Within Keynesian theory, investment finance is distinguished from saving. But money, which finances investment, performs additional functions, most notably the provision of liquidity when expected returns on alternative assets are low or particularly uncertain. The cost and availability of investment finance are thus determined by liquidity preference (as well as the demand for investment finance) relative to the willingness of financial institutions to extend credit, which in turn is influenced by their own liquidity preference. Planned saving can influence the outcome in the sense that planned investment is influenced by expectations of consumer demand (or derived demand for capital goods) and that the behaviour of financial institutions (and particularly the term structure of interest rates) will be influenced by the disposition of additions to wealth as well as the existing stock of wealth. But the volume of planned saving as such has no direct bearing on the question. (See Asimakopoulos 1983,1985, 1986a and 1986b, Suppe 1985, Mott 1985-86, Davidson 1986, Kregel 1986 and Richardson 1986 for a difference of opinion on this subject.)

This interpretation of Keynesian monetary theory, then, is more complex than the Kaldorian version of uniform national financial conditions. The regional level of planned investment is still the key to regional employment and output. But investment plans are seen as only one upshot of sets of expectations which also generate the state of liquidity preference and the behaviour of financial institutions, all of which are likely to vary from region to region.

We proceed now to a more detailed outline of Keynesian monetary theory as applied to economies experiencing different economic conditions over time. The framework within which this outline is expressed is Chick's (1986) characterisation of the historical stages of banking. The translation of this purely temporal theory into a spatial context (albeit in historical time) is attempted in section three.

2.2 KEYNESIAN MONETARY THEORY WITHIN THE CONTEXT OF BANKING DEVELOPMENT

The coexistence, outlined above, of competing theories as to the primacy of investment over saving, or vice versa, can be understood in terms of different stages of banking development. In these terms, the primacy of saving is a reasonable hypothesis for the earliest period of banking development, but not for subsequent banking practice. Mainstream theorists who persist in identifying investment finance with saving have thus not allowed for institutional change, as indeed is to be expected on the basis of an ahistorical, universalist theoretical method.

Chick (1986) traces the stages of development of banking systems, outlining the type of monetary theory relevant to each stage. This framework in turn encourages a fresh look at contemporary banking, identifying a new stage in the 1970s and 1980s and thus a different type of monetary theory from that relevant to previous decades. (See also Chick and Dow, 1988.)

The first stage refers to the earliest period of banking, during which banks act purely as intermediaries between savers and investors, but their liabilities do not constitute a means of payment. It is this stage alone in which saving is necessarily prior to investment.

Once bank notes and/or deposits are used as money, in the second stage, the redeposit ratio from bank lending will be high. Banks can then go beyond the first stage of simply lending out deposits. Given an initial deposit (or addition to reserves) banks lend out a multiple of this amount, financing investment, 'creating' deposits, and generating income and saving.

The third stage of banking development sees the development of interbank lending. Individual banks, lending in excess of the initial reserves increase, can now do so more readily. If loans do not lead to redeposits quickly enough for an individual bank to meet its reserve requirements, interbank lending can bridge the gap. The result is a more rapid multiplier process, bringing forward the availability of investment finance and speeding up the income generation process. The final total of credit creation is still dependent on the available stock of bank reserves.

The capacity of banks to meet the demand for investment finance is enhanced even further in the fourth stage, which sees the emergence of a central bank or lender-of-last-resort. The stock of bank reserves is now responsive to demand from the banks. Banks collectively expanding credit can thus do so without risk of being caught short of reserves, if the central bank stands ready to make up any shortfall. The salutary effect this facility has on bankers' expectations is further enhanced if the central bank has a stable interest rate policy; in such a situation, the supply of reserves and their price are both assured. The demand for bank loans at that interest rate (plus a margin) fully determines their supply, and thus the supply of deposits.

Chick identifies a further, fifth, stage, reached in the 1970s, where banks are no longer passive in the face of the demand for advances, but actively seek both lending opportunities *and* deposits. The driving force in the expansion of investment finance and the volume of deposits is thus now the banks' aggressive struggle for increased market share. In turn, the resulting jacking-up of interest rates on deposits requires correspondingly increased returns on advances and thus on the expenditure they finance. The survival of the financial system in such circumstances requires an escalation of asset prices, i.e. inflation.

We wish here to apply these ideas within a regional context, where economic conditions vary across regions. However, it is instructive to consider first how financial variables influence economic activity within a

13

single economy over time, as its economic conditions change. Indeed Keynes' theory was one 'of why output and employment are so liable to fluctuation' (Keynes 1936, p.221), so that the full flavour of his theory becomes apparent only in the context of changing economic conditions (see Minsky 1975, chapter 3).

A theme which runs through the Keynesian theory of monetary production is that decision-making with respect (inevitably) to the future involves uncertainty of a fundamental kind. (See Keynes 1937.) Uncertainty differs from risk in that it prevents the quantification of expectations; it reflects, further, the degree of confidence with which any expectation is held. Some expectations may be held with a high degree of confidence if they derive from an unchanging structure; actuarial expectations fall into this category. But in general the structure within which investment planning takes place is susceptible to changes of an unpredictable sort: changes in behaviour, in institutional arrangements, in economic conditions, in products and technology, and in other agents' expectations. In order to deal with this uncertainty, investors conform to group conventions as a guide to behaviour. There will thus be conventional expectations about the state of the economy, the availability of external finance, etc. These conventions are subjective, but only in the sense that there is no complete objective basis for decision-making. This, then, is the background against which we must consider the influence of financial variables on investment within different institutional structures.

In the first of Chick's stages, investment expenditure is dependent on the availability (through the intermediation of the banks) of others' savings, or of retained earnings. In the absence of usury laws, the interest rate would be determined by the availability of saving relative to investment demand. Nevertheless, investment would be the driving force particularly in an expansion, with saving the constraint. If the economy is buoyant, justifying payment of a relatively high interest rate on borrowed funds, banks would be able to attract more deposits, allowing more investment to go ahead. New income growth and thus saving growth would accordingly be generated, putting downward pressure on the interest rate and encouraging even more investment. Conversely, a wave of pessimism which reduces

14

investors' plans to use available saving would generate reduced income growth, and thus saving growth, eventually putting upward pressure on the interest rate, further discouraging investment. In both cases, the cumulative process is slow. In the case of expansion, investors must at each stage wait for saving to emerge to finance the next investment project. In the case of contraction, the rate of interest will only rise once the pool of unused saving is used up.

As the banking system develops, and investment is financed in anticipation of saving, the process of expansion and decline is speeded up. Now, in the case of expansion, investors can borrow on the strength of their expectations of good returns (if these are shared by the banks), with the consequent income growth allowing absorption of the corresponding increase in deposits. In the second and third stages, there must still be an initial injection of bank reserves from some source (such as increased exports) to back the expansion of credit, but banks are free to expand credit as a multiple of these reserves. In the case of contraction, investors find their expectations disappointed and thus experience difficulty in repaying loans without curtailing planned expenditure, causing multiple contraction in income, saving and bank deposits, although not necessarily of bank reserves (unless, for example, falling exports are a feature of the contraction).

Not only are investment plans still the driving force of expansions and contractions, but saving plans as such no longer constrain investment. Within the constraint of available bank reserves, the cost and availability of finance are determined rather by the willingness of banks and other financial institutions to finance business investment in view of their own expectations of business conditions, but also in view of their expectations as to the returns on alternative assets. For alongside the growing capacity of banks to extend credit, as a multiple of reserves, there is a growing sophistication in the markets for alternative financial instruments (particularly government securities) which offer alternative opportunities for profit-making. By the third stage, too, when interbank lending is developed, individual banks are less constrained by reserves availability, although the overall banking system is still constrained by aggregate reserves.

15

Before the emergence of a lender-of-last-resort facility, i.e. before the fourth stage, banks are very vulnerable to economy-wide fluctuations. In the case of a contraction, growing uncertainty about the viability of investment projects (and thus default risk) would encourage banks to concentrate more on readily tradeable financial securities, i.e. to make their portfolios more liquid. At the same time, however, wealth holders would also aim for more liquidity in anticipation of falling prices of non-money assets, thus driving down their price. The combined effect of these financial developments, alongside business investors' own long-run expectations, is to discourage investment by raising the cost of credit, reducing its availability, and lowering the expected return on the investment itself. Further, individual banks experiencing a severe reserves drain may themselves find it more difficult to attract credit, leading to bank failure. Correspondingly, in a more expansionary climate, low liquidity preference on the part of financial institutions and the non-bank sector increase the availability of credit and reduce its cost, as businesses plan to increase investment. Such an expansionary climate is conducive too to the emergence of new financial instruments and financial institutions.

Financial and business investors are governed by different priorities and different sets of expectations. Keynes (1936, chapter 12) identifies financial investors, or 'speculators', who are concerned with short-run fluctuations in the prices of financial assets in an attempt to buy cheap and sell dear. The resulting price and yield on tradeable financial assets thus determine the cost of business finance from this source. But the demand for business credit, on the part of 'entrepreneurs', reflects long-term considerations about the viability of physical investment projects. Further, the supply of investment finance from the alternative source, the banks, depends on the banks' state of liquidity preference, i.e. their preference for tradeable financial assets rather than business loans.

Indeed, the more active financial markets become, the more credit will be demanded to finance activity in these markets rather than 'productive' activity. Keynes (1936, chapter 22) argued that, during business expansions, prices of non-reproducible (speculative) assets accelerate, eventually offering a higher return than could feasibly be expected from business investment. Speculative activity could thus 'crowd out' productive activity even before full employment is reached. Further, the more expansive the speculative bubble, the more dramatic its bursting, i.e. the more constrained will be the availability of finance for any purpose during the downturn.

How far this process is reinforced or curtailed during the fourth stage depends on the behaviour of the monetary authorities. If a stable interest rate policy is maintained regardless of economic conditions, the scope for illiquidity in the downturn phase is limited; in addition the danger of productive activity during the expansionary phase being crowded out is reduced. If, however, monetary authorities resort to the temptation to raise interest rates to curtail a speculative boom, the likely effect is to divert more funds from productive to unproductive uses, contributing to financial instability, as well as instability of output and employment.

Chick argues that in the current, fifth, stage, trade in financial assets has broken away from the cycle in output and employment as a result of the unconstrained activities of banks. Liability management involves banks attempting to attract deposits (with high interest rates) throughout the cycle, matching loans for speculative activity. A counter-cyclical pattern in liquidity preference in earlier stages implied a counter-cyclical pattern in willingness to hold bank deposits. Now, Chick argues, liquidity preference is satisfied by currency movements, i.e. by switching between the liabilities of different economies. This spatial aspect of liquidity preference hints at an application to regional economies. Further, for earlier stages in banking development, where the total amount of credit creation is constrained by reserves availability, the regional distribution of the total is clearly of great importance for regional economic development. In the following section we attempt to translate this version of Keynesian monetary theory into regional terms.

2.3 A REGIONAL VERSION OF KEYNESIAN MONETARY THEORY

A temporal theory does not have an automatic spatial equivalent. But there are aspects of the theory set out above which lend themselves to a regional interpretation. Indeed, the first stage of banking corresponds to the orthodox mainstream version of regional monetary theory. Regional financial flows are the result of intermediation between savers in one region and investors in another. The larger the pool of savings on which regional investors may draw, the more investment there will be in the regions where domestic savings fall short of investment. On the other hand, investment will be correspondingly reduced in regions with plentiful savings if the increased competition for funds, from other regions, deters local investors.

In terms of dependency theory, it is the Centre type of region, with its wealth, which invests in the Periphery type of region, with its investment opportunities. The yield from Periphery growth thus adds to Centre wealth; the increased level of economic activity in Periphery is at the cost of growing dependency on Centre for export markets and finance, and a growing disparity in development between the two types of region. If there is a high import content to the investment expenditure, the income multiplier will be low, as will savings growth and the redeposit ratio in Periphery financial institutions. The resulting volatility of deposits in Periphery banks will make these banks very vulnerable to bankruptcy. The pressure therefore will be towards banking concentration, with national banks enjoying a competitive advantage over local banks in the Periphery.

Once bank deposits and/or notes begin to be treated as money, in stage two, the traditional bank multiplier theory applies with credit creation constrained by bank reserves rather than saving; this has special significance for regions. Regional banks' capacity to extend credit depends both on the size of the multiplier, and on the multiplicand, which may vary systematically by region. The multiplier is greater the lower the cash/deposit ratio and the propensities to import and to invest outside the region, while the multiplicand is determined by new reserves from the central bank, or net deposit increases as a result of interregional payments in the initial period. (See Dow 1982.)

If banking is regionally distinct, then credit creation in each region is constrained by the regional banks' reserves; regional differences in reserves growth will depend on regional differences in trade and capital flows. But once, by stage three, banks extend credit to each other across regions, some of these interregional flows may constitute inter-bank transfers. As a result, a reserves shortage on the part of any one region's banks may be made up by credit from banks in other regions with an excess of reserves. If, further,

18

banks branch interregionally, these flows will occur within, as well as between, banks, further reducing the dependence on regional bank reserves for regional credit creation.

The cause of changes in regional reserves, as manifested in the regional balance of payments, nevertheless remains of central importance in reflecting both regional investment opportunities and the banks' willingness to finance them, although the relationship is now more complex. If a region's balance of payments is in deficit (and local banks' reserves falling) because of imports of capital goods and raw materials for new production which will eventually generate increased exports, then extra-regional bank credit will be attracted by high prospective returns. If, however, the deficit is due to declining exports, extra-regional bank credit is less likely to be forthcoming because of default risk, and so the region's banks' reserves constraint will be binding on credit creation within the region.

When considering the locational pattern of banking concentration, it is reasonable to assume that the banking centre emerges in whatever region is dominant, or Central, at the early stages of banking development. (See Kindleberger 1974.) The Centre region, then, has a concentration of the country's wealth, proximity to the financial decision-making centre, and most ready access to markets in all financial instruments and innovations in the functioning of those markets.

As long as investment opportunities are perceived to have higher yields in the Periphery than in the Centre, banks will extend credit there more readily than to Centre projects. But the early pattern of Centre wealth consistently financing the opening of economic frontiers in the Periphery must now be modified. First, the more decision-making occurs in head offices in the Centre (as in a branch-banking system) the more information problems are likely to arise in terms of perceptions of relative yields, and particularly of default risk. Long-term expectations of bank managers, like those of entrepreneurs, must rely significantly on group conventions. The more remote the relevant group is from first-hand information, the more unreliable those conventional expectations will be. Not only will this concentration in banking lead to more mistakes (in retrospect) in investment financing decisions, but it will tend to encourage industrial concentration; the best information available

19

to bank head offices will come from head offices of nationwide corporations located also in the Centre. (Sociological considerations would add an extra dimension to the significance of personal contacts among businessmen and bankers in the Centre for the formation of conventional expectations and the allocation of credit.)

But in addition, the relative liquidity preference on the part of different groups influences the provision of investment finance, as well as the demand for it. An important characteristic of dependent, Peripheral economies is that they are more strongly cyclical than dominant, Central economies. This inherent instability may itself discourage investment finance from outside institutions. But it would eventually lead to particular caution on the part of local institutions against over-extension in local assets; this would be true of all sectors in the Peripheral economy, but more especially of financial institutions. This suggests that, on average, liquidity preference will be higher the more unstable the economy. This liquidity preference will be satisfied by deposits in nationwide, rather than local banks, and by national rather than local securities. This tendency would be particularly marked as soon as any doubts emerged about the viability of a boom phase. This tendency for short-term and medium term capital outflows from Periphery to Centre is bound to be exacerbated by the greater financial sophistication of the Centre financial markets. A further manifestation of Periphery's higher liquidity preference would be a higher cash-deposit ratio and a higher reserve ratio for local financial institutions, i.e. a lower deposit multiplier.

Overall, then, to the extent that banking is regionally distinct, credit creation in Peripheral regions will tend to be lower than for Central regions, due to a lower multiplier and a lower multiplicand. The only countervailing force is perceived high returns and low default risk on Periphery investments. But, if there is no such clear-cut attraction of Periphery investment over Centre investment, the overall allocation of credit, given the banking system's reserve base, will tend to favour Centre projects. Further, branches of national banks will have a competitive advantage over local, Periphery banks, because of the absence of a strict reserves constraint, so that there will be an inherent tendency towards banking concentration. Then, regional credit creation is no longer constrained by regional bank reserves. But, even then, the perceived value to the national banks of Periphery credit must be relatively high to justify inter-branch transfers to finance it. If the regional balance of payments is in deficit (i.e. reserves are falling) because of falling exports and a lack of confidence in the region's assets, then national banks will be unwilling to extend credit within the region (and indeed there may be little demand for it for more investment). The reserves constraint is then simply internalised within the bank.

Once the banking system reaches stage four, it is no longer constrained by a particular reserve base at the national level either; the central bank stands ready to meet demand. The only limit to bank credit expansion is now its willingness to meet demand for credit at the interest rate maintained by the monetary authorities. Now, regional credit creation is no longer a matter of the allocation of a given national total of reserves. Credit expansion can now occur in regions with relatively high expected returns without inter-bank or inter-branch borrowing of reserves. Credit creation in the former regions need no longer occur 'at the expense of' credit creation in the regions providing the reserves. Regional credit creation will now be determined by the regional demand for credit (derived from investment plans and/or the need for borrowed working capital, relative to other opportunities), the banks' willingness to extend the credit, and the terms attached to the credit derived from national monetary policy.

The regional demand for credit and the banks' willingness to supply it (where willingness refers both to availability and position in the national interest rate structure) will reflect perceptions of regional economic conditions on the part of local entrepreneurs and of the financial institutions, and the state of regional liquidity preference. Each of these factors has a strong regional dimension, even though, by this stage of banking development, it is no longer relevant to consider regional credit allocation in terms of the distribution of a given stock of bank reserves. Investment plans, credit availability and terms, and asset choice in general are still the outcome of comparisons between alternative opportunities; in a regional context, the closest alternatives include those available in other regions.

For regional entrepreneurs, local investment opportunities arise from a situation of regional interdependence. Opportunities in Peripheral regions

21

which tend to be dominated by primary production are dependent on the state of their markets in Central regions. Perceptions of these opportunities on the part of financial institutions in turn reflect the state of knowledge on the part of these institutions both with respect to Peripheral economies and with respect to the borrowers themselves. Further, any increase in liquidity preference in Peripheral regions causing capital flight will thereby simply reduce regional liquidity and depress asset prices, and thus the value of collateral against which credit might be extended to ease the lack of liquidity.

In short, the availability of borrowed reserves from a central monetary authority does not mean that the supply of credit for any borrower or group of borrowers is unlimited. Indeed the supply of credit is likely to conform to the same type of regional pattern as outlined for earlier stages of the banking system. But that pattern is now likely to be even more marked, with credit creation in both Peripheral and Central regions more unconstrained during boom conditions. Their boom conditions are unlikely to coincide however, those in Peripheral regions deriving from raw material booms and those in Central regions from speculative (financial) booms.

Although the regional distribution of bank reserves ceased to be a direct constraint on regional credit creation once banks lent reserves across regions (between banks or branches of the same bank), it still has some importance even when national reserves are unconstrained. The reserves of individual banks, or those imputed to individual branches, correspond to new deposits. With unconstrained credit creation, the new deposits in general *follow* from credit creation. But the *net* addition to deposits depends on the propensity for new credit to be expended on imports or extra-regional assets (or repayment of extra-regional debt). Low deposit growth relative to lending growth in particular regions (or, indeed, branches), if it is perceived as persistent, is generally a signal for credit creation to be cut back.

In the current, fifth, stage of banking development, banks actively seek both investment opportunities and deposits; the latter is achieved by raising deposit rates, and thus loan rates. Investment opportunities for which credit is created will thus require ever higher expected returns. Lending activity will accordingly be concentrated in growth industries and in speculative assets; for other sectors, increasing borrowing costs will squeeze profitability unless producers have sufficient market control to pass the costs on in higher prices. To the extent that Peripheral regions are dependent on industries not currently growing and/or with a large number of small producers, higher borrowing costs will exacerbate their liquidity problems; financial speculation, which will attract a high proportion of credit creation since its profitability is endogenous to the financial sector, will be concentrated in the financial centre. Thus this final stage sees a further exaggeration of the earlier regional pattern of more volatile credit creation in Peripheral regions than Central regions (reflecting cycles in primary production) a higher liquidity preference in Peripheral regions, satisfied by capital outflows to Central regions, and a general pattern of credit creation which encourages large, national investors, who have better access to credit lines in the financial centre, and more market power to pass on rising interest costs. Now the regional pattern of bank reserves is purely notional, but the forces which lead to interregional payments imbalance (i.e. changes in notional regional reserves) are still of primary importance in determining the regional pattern of credit demand and its supply.

2.4 CONCLUSION

The stages approach to banking development allows us to construct hypotheses about the impact of financial variables on regional economic development. In the early stages of banking development, we are concerned with a relatively straightforward issue of allocation, with savings, and then bank reserves, being directed towards regions experiencing high expected returns on investment. But the allocation decisions are made progressively in the financial centre (generally the location of old wealth), as financial institutions become more concentrated, attracting the assets of those seeking liquidity. Financial concentration in turn encourages concentration in production via the increasingly centralised process of credit creation. At the early stages of financial development, the financial constraints on investment will be particularly strong when investment opportunities are plentiful, and the regional distribution of scarce finance will be a keen issue.

Branch banking and the availability of a lender of last resort facility remove the absolute reserves constraint on regional credit creation. Lending in any region can then be expanded on the strength of reserves borrowed from the central bank (rather than other regions). But the factors which determine the net deposit creation resulting from credit creation for any region (which would earlier have determined the regional reserves constraint) will still be important as determinants of further credit creation. Credit creation will still be unconstrained if a tendency to deficit is temporary, but not if it is an indicator of economic stagnation. As the financial sector in general becomes more developed, the tendency for Periphery deposits to be eroded by capital outflows to the Centre will be exacerbated, regardless of the state of the Periphery economy relative to Centre, but particularly during periods of especially high liquidity preference in Periphery. The regional pattern of liquidity preference will become a progressively more important factor in regional credit creation, influencing perceptions of returns from the uses of credit, as the financial sector becomes more sophisticated. This tendency becomes even more marked as banks become more aggressive in seeking deposits and loan opportunities, raising financial returns relative to returns on production.

The net result, then, that we would expect to see is that credit creation in Periphery will be attracted by boom conditions in its primary sector, but be cut back sharply once that boom starts to deflate, as a result of capital outflows and/or falls in asset prices not likely to be reversed in the near future. The Centre economy will not experience financial constraints of the same order and will accordingly not experience the same degree of liquidity preference during recessions; any increase in liquidity preference in any case, would tend to be satisfied by assets issued in Centre. Although the regional reserves constraint is no longer binding on regional credit creation, the other aspects of financial development described here (financial and industrial concentration, and the growing importance of liquidity preference and the regional aspects of its satisfaction) will ensure a continued asymmetry in regional credit creation, and thus in regional development.

In the next chapter, we look at the history of the Canadian financial system from the point of view of its regional impact, to see how far it conforms to the pattern outlined above. The following chapter will attempt to assess the theory

24

more explicitly with respect to the fourth and fifth stages of banking development, i.e. during the last twenty years or so for which detailed regional data have been available for Canada.

3 Canadian financial history from a regional perspective

3.1 INTRODUCTION

Chapter two contained a stylised account of the historical development of banking systems. What was highlighted was the growing capacity of the banks to extend credit, as financial institutions and behaviour evolve over time. The precise content, and indeed sequencing, of the five stages will vary from one financial system to another, depending on the structure of the economy, the legislative framework and the pattern of financial behaviour that these encourage or allow. In this chapter we attempt to make the analysis more concrete by referring to a particular financial history, that of Canada.

In the next section we start with a description of the banking system as it developed, region by region. It is shown how each region fared with respect to credit creation in terms of the stages of banking development relative to stages of economic development. As each region is discussed, mention is made of the analysis of credit creation typical of each region, and of the actions of the relevant provincial governments to overcome actual or perceived constraints.

The banks, however, are not the sole source of credit, although they have been unique in the moneyness of their liabilities (and thus their high redeposit ratios) and in their access to the Bank of Canada as lender-of-last resort. But, on the banking system as base there has been built a structure of non-bank financial intermediaries which can create credit to the extent that their redeposit ratios and their resources (bank deposits) allow them. With financial development has gone a dramatic increase in the non-bank financial sector growing from rough equality with the banking sector until the 1950s to three times the banking sector by 1970 (see Neufeld 1972, Appendix Table A). The moneyness of non-bank liabilities has increased as, for example, trust companies have introduced demand deposits and chequing facilities. As a result, the banks have increasingly found themselves in competition with the non-banks for deposits, a significant feature of the current, fifth stage of banking development with its drive for market share.

In general, although the earlier discussion was conducted in terms of the banks only, the general principles expounded still hold once we extend consideration to the non-banks, and indeed are reinforced. The banks' growing capacity to extend credit, and freedom to allocate it among regions is reinforced by a similar capacity among a growing non-bank sector. For completeness, then, we include in sections three to six a discussion (in regional terms) of the historical development of savings banks, caisses populaires and credit unions, mortgage loan companies, trust companies, pension companies, mutual funds and investment companies.

The financial system at the national level was dependent for its resources in the early stages of development on foreign exchange. In addition, banking behaviour and legislation were influenced by Canada's economic and political ties with Britain, France and the United States. Since the national situation set the constraints on credit creation in the different regions, particularly in their early stages of economic development, section seven is devoted to a discussion of the external influences on Canada's financial system.

Provincial governments have responded specifically to the question of how financial institutions (particularly banks) have affected their economies. Their analyses and policy measures are integrated into the region-by-region discussion below. The federal government's analysis, as expressed in various Royal Commission Reports, is also touched on. However, most

27

federal measures specifically addressed to regional questions have been of a fiscal rather than financial nature. These are outlined briefly in the final section.

3.2 THE BANKING SYSTEM

Canada's financial system evolved as part and parcel of the settlement and economic development of each region. On the one hand this evolution was influenced by the currency and credit needs of trade in the major staple products; as a result the chartered banks saw their primary function as being the provision of trade credit rather than industrial, residential or consumer credit. (See Easterbrook and Aitken 1956, chapter 19.) On the other hand, it was influenced by the example set by banking systems developed elsewhere, particularly in England and Scotland;[1] the result was a high degree of caution in lending, a caution not necessarily appropriate for a country at Canada's stage of development when the banking system developed.

Prior to the appearance of a banking system, currency consisted of a motley collection of coins, supplemented by various experimental issues of paper money by the colonial governments. In the North and West, the Hudson's Bay Company used adult male beaver skins in prime condition as the standard of value and issued tokens called made-beavers, and indeed the Company performed intermediation functions for its employees. Credit to finance the harvesting of fur and timber until payment was received was provided by companies in the importing country.

As trade and economic activity expanded, however, the need for a locally-based source of currency and credit increased. It was the Canadian merchants themselves who formed the first banks, financing trade credit by issuing notes for the use of the local population, raising the Canadian financial system into the second of Chick's stages of development. The bank charters issued by the appropriate territorial governments took a broadly common form. The main features were the limitation of note issues to the value of some multiple of paid up capital, plus deposits, and a prohibition on mortgage lending; banks could however establish their own reserves rules and open branches.

28

The regional pattern of chartered bank formation and closure can be gleaned from Table 3.1, showing the number of charters granted and acted upon, the number of banks taken over or merged and the number of failures, up to 1986, with the time-span of each of these events in parentheses. The number of banks extant in 1986, shown in the last column, totalled nine. The data are shown by area, using the names of provinces as they are now. (During the period of bank formation, Quebec was first Lower Canada, then Canada East. Ontario was first Upper Canada, then Canada West.)

3.2.1 The Atlantic Region

Banking started roughly contemporaneously in New Brunswick, Quebec, Ontario and Nova Scotia in the 1820s.[2] The chartered banking system in the four Atlantic provinces operated more or less independently of the rest of the country until close to the turn of the century. Newfoundland's two banks both collapsed in 1894, whereupon four central Canadian banks opened up branches on the island, and the local currency was tied to the Canadian dollar. (Newfoundland did not join Confederation until 1949.) The other three Atlantic provinces experienced a decline in economic conditions relative to the rest of Canada from the 1860s, which accelerated as new opportunities opened up in the West. Eleven banks failed and the remainder attempted to protect their positions with mergers. But six takeovers by banks outside the region, the removal of the Merchants Bank of Halifax to Montreal under the new name of the Royal Bank of Canada, and the consolidation of the remaining banks in the Bank of Nova Scotia, meant that, by the outbreak of World War I, only the Bank of Nova Scotia remained, and even then the General Manager's office had been moved to Toronto. The Canadian banking system moved into the third stage of development with regional credit creation not limited to local reserves, more by means of the development of branch banking than the development of inter-bank credit.

The gradual absorption of Maritime banking, at the end of the nineteenth century, into a national banking network centred in Toronto and Montreal coincided with the opening up of the West with large capital needs for the

Table 3.1

Chartered Banks (active) by Province of Head Office 1820-1986[a]

	Number of Charters Used[b]		Number Taken Over[c]		Number Collapsed[d]		Number Extant
Newfoundland	2	(1854-8)	-		2	(1894)	-
Nova Scotia	11	(1832-73)	6	(1901-1910)	4	(1873-1905)	1
Prince Edward I	4	(1860-71)	3	(1883-1906)	1	(1892)	-
New Brunswick	9	(1820-72)	3	(1839-1913)	6	(1837-1910)	-
Quebec	29	(1822-1979)	15	(1876-1985)	11	(1831-1908)	3
Ontario	37	(1821-1977)	18	(1840-1977)	16	(1840-1923)	3
Manitoba	4	(1885-1908)	3	(1908-25)	1	(1893)	0
Saskatchewan	1	(1910)	1	(1931)	-		-
Alberta	3	(1975-84)	-		2	(1985)	1
British Columbia	5	(1862-1984)	3	(1900-86)	1	(1914)	1

a The relevant time-span is shown in parentheses.
b A total of 61 charters were issued but not used.
c Includes mergers and those which received charters under a new name as a result of merger or movement of head office.
d Includes those whose charters were revoked.

Source: C.S. Howard (1950) and updated with reference to recent publications of the new chartered banks.

financing of the railroads and, later, wheat and mining. There was then a generally-held perception that funds were being drawn out of the Maritimes by the chartered banks, to be lent out at high interest rates in the West, and by the federal government savings bank to finance the Canadian Pacific Railway. Naylor quoted Edmund Walker of the Bank of Commerce, describing Maritimes objections to this process, in 1913, as 'local grievances against what we regard as the interests of the country as a whole, (see Naylor, 1975, p.103); Walker did not deny the Maritimers' perception of capital outflow. Further, negotiations for Newfoundland's entry into Confederation are said by MacKay (1946) to have been seriously set back by resentment against the Toronto and Montreal banks; they had opened branches in Newfoundland on the demise of the two local banks, and then refused to extend credit to the Newfoundland Savings Bank, which was facing closure.

The 'Maritime problem' of deindustrialisation, and a falling-behind in incomes and employment relative to the rest of Canada from the turn of the century, were not necessarily the result of 'real' forces in the sense of a long-run fall in competitiveness. The traditional picture is one of an economy on the brink of decline, which had no choice but to be taken over by more prosperous enterprises in Central Canada. Acheson (1977) and Brym and Sacouman (1979, Introduction) describe it rather as a reasonably healthy economy in 'real' terms which did not however have the financial resources to resist takeover and whose industry was then successively closed down as the Central Canadian parents attempted to rationalize their operations and to drive out any remaining competition.[3] Acheson suggests that the centralisation of activity was the inevitable outcome of the National Party, which attempted to integrate the entire Canadian economy as a viable competitor in the international setting.

Dependency theorists such as Brym and Sacouman go further in pointing to the inevitability of disparities in economic development under capitalism, both within the Maritimes and between the Maritimes and the rest of Canada. The channelling of local savings out of rural areas in the Maritimes and out of the region altogether by corporations and financial institutions is regarded by some as an inherent part of the process.[4] This view of the rôle of financial institutions in the Atlantic region, however, has not found expression in a

31

political movement in the same way as it has in Quebec and Western Canada.[5]

Proposals for financial reform emerging from the Maritimes have tended to start from the position that the Maritime Economy has fallen behind the rest of Canada. While there may be a comparative advantage in some staples industries, a catching-up in incomes and employment requires the development of a strong manufacturing sector (and, more recently, high-return energy-related staples). Whatever may be the historical reasons for the Maritimes' disadvantaged state, growth in many manufacturing industries requires a start from scratch with new small businesses, which have particular financial needs. Not having retained earnings, new businesses require medium and long-term loans in the initial stages, while banks provide predominantly short-term loans. Also, since the Atlantic region is perceived to be risky for new enterprise, on the basis of past experience, those institutions specialising in longer-term loans (trust companies and insurance companies) tend to favour large, established businesses with good collateral. Requests for Bank of Canada directives to the banks to allocate more credit to the Maritimes were repeatedly turned down in the late 1950s. (See Lounsbury 1960, pp.216-28, and Cairncross 1961, pp.3-6). Lending agencies were however set up by the Atlantic provincial governments, and federal agencies' terms of reference were broadened, so that by the 1960s a major financing gap was being filled by the public sector.

The question still was being posed, however, whether the banks were unfairly discriminating against borrowers in the Maritimes, and not responding to local needs. (The strength of feeling against banks headquartered elsewhere is evident from the fact that the Bank of Nova Scotia maintains its head office nominally in Halifax, although almost all head office functions are performed in Toronto.) A background paper prepared for the Royal Commission on Canada's Economic Prospects by Hood (1958) concluded that, for Canada as a whole, financial institutions were unable to meet satisfactorily the financial requirements of small business.[6] Lounsbury (1960), in his report for the Atlantic Provinces Research Board, reiterated this conclusion for the Maritimes, where there is a relatively high incidence of small businesses. He did however argue that the Atlantic provinces benefitted from having access to a sound national banking system, backed by assets in the rest of Canada.

Three studies have assessed the charge of inadequate bank financing, by means of questioning business managers in the Atlantic provinces: Cairncross (1961), Sears (1972) for Nova Scotia only, and Benton (1974) for the Atlantic Provinces Economic Council. While all conclude that there is no conclusive evidence of unsatisfied demand for credit among the established businesses they surveyed, Sears and Benton identified inadequacies for manufacturing businesses and new and or small business. Sears' study suggests that these inadequacies stem primarily from inadequate training of bank personnel in assessing the viability of new enterprises (many of which are in the manufacturing sector). Since evaluation of character was being used as the primary criterion of credit-worthiness, the natural risk-aversion of bankers was given a subjective outlet for expression.[7] In any case, even if it were justified by normal banking practice, it should be a matter for concern if there is inadequate provision of finance precisely for those types of firm which are normally regarded as the engine of growth. Further, it is difficult using survey methods to identify demand for loans which was not made effective, either because the business never got off the ground due to lack of finance, or because the borrower was deterred by unfavourable terms, or pessimism about the likely outcome, from making a loan application.

Whether justified or not, many borrowers or potential borrowers are viewed by the banks as marginal because of high perceived risk. During times of tight national monetary policy, Maritime credit is reduced disproportionately (see Lounsbury 1960). Cairncross (1961) suggests that this may be due to the fact that risk may increase disproportionately when monetary policy is tight because of the interest-sensitivity of the market for Maritime products. However he questioned the suitability of tight monetary policy for an economy almost perpetually underemployed. He pointed to examples in other countries of regional differences in the implementation of tight monetary policy and recommended that the Bank of Canada use moral suasion to exempt Atlantic borrowers from credit restrictions. Cairncross did however view regional monetary policy as having only limited potential within a nationwide financial system. He suggests that contracting credit was more a result of contracting demand than supply; policy could more effectively be focused on encouraging investment by direct incentives rather than monetary policy. Passaris (1975, 1976, 1977) nevertheless continued to outline the damage done by national monetary policy to Maritimes investment, and to make the case for a differentiated regional monetary policy.

3.2.2 Ontario and Quebec

The chartering of new banks has throughout the period had the highest incidence in Ontario and Quebec. Some chartered banks failed up to 1910, but the proportionate number of failures was less than in the Atlantic region. Ontario's early charters allowed state purchase of shares up to one-fifth of paid-up capital in the case of the Bank of Upper Canada. Indeed the directorship of the Bank of Upper Canada, the first significant bank (chartered in 1821), was dominated by politicians. There was considerable rivalry between this bank, the financial arm of what was called the 'Family Compact' and the Bank of Montreal, the financial arm of the Montreal merchants dubbed the 'Chateau Clique'. This rivalry was resolved in 1866 when the Bank of Upper Canada folded as a result of excessive lending on security of land by-passed by the new railroad developments. The Bank of Montreal had by then taken over as the province of Canada's bank, and continued to perform limited central banking functions until the Bank of Canada was set up.

The Bank of Upper Canada had been able to exert sufficient political influence to limit the granting of charters in Ontario, in spite of the rapidly growing demand for credit, particularly from farmers. Several applicants for charters resorted to setting up private banks instead, i.e. banks without charter, and thus without legislative restriction except with respect to the issue of small notes. The financial crisis of 1836-9 and its restrictive legislative aftermath forced most of them to close. Private banks were also formed in Quebec during this period.

The financial crisis (imported from Britain and the United States) forced most banks temporarily to suspend payment of specie on their notes. As a result greater caution was urged on them by the British authorities. The term of credit was shortened, with more serious consequences for farmers (with seasonal credit needs) than for traders (for whom shipments were becoming more speedy and efficient). Private banks were prohibited from issuing notes of denomination less than five pounds (then equivalent to twenty dollars at the official rate of exchange), effectively driving them out of note issuing. A circulation tax of 1% was imposed on the chartered banks' note issue. There were proposals considered at this time for the government to have sole right of issue, through its own bank, and for other means of direct control of the money supply. The banks however succeeded in resisting these proposals and government involvement in note issue did not occur until 1866, and even then only in a marginal way.

The only other attempt to alter the basis of note issue at that time was the Free Banking Act of 1850, which provided for small banks (with no branching facilities) which would issue notes of small denomination backed one-hundred per cent by government securities. The Act took as its model the unit banking system in New York State, and appealed to the Reformist movement which had pressed for the freeing-up of the banking system in the 1830s. Few banks however were formed under the Act and it was repealed in 1880. The attractions of the only partial backing of note issue enjoyed by the chartered banks (ten per cent of paid-up capital in government securities) as well as the branching facility made chartered banking too appealing an alternative for most new entrants into the banking industry.

The British North America Act of 1867 assigned to the federal government the control of coinage, currency and banking. Banking legislation, as well as the facility to open branches, was extended nationwide. The banks' capacity to issue notes was restricted to the value of paid-up capital, and only in denominations of four dollars or more (increased subsequently to five dollars). The Dominion note issue (partially backed by gold) which now monopolised one dollar and two dollar notes was increased and banks were required to hold one-third of their reserves in Dominion notes. The chartered banks continued to issue their own notes until 1945 and the last notes were removed from circulation in 1950.

By the end of the First World War, Canadian banking was concentrated to such an extent that all head offices or management offices were in Ontario or Quebec, with the one exception of the Weyburn Security Bank in Saskatchewan which remained independent until 1931. By then, the banks were down to ten, four with head offices in Ontario and five in Quebec, and the Bank of Nova Scotia's titular head office in Halifax. Restrictions on note issue had reduced the elasticity of the money supply in response to demand. Various measures were thus taken to ease the situation. From 1908, temporary excess note issues were allowed over the summer to finance the movement of crops. Then in 1914, the Finance Act provided for bank borrowing of Dominion notes. The government thus effectively returned to the banks the initiative in determining the total note issue.

But the (Macmillan) Royal Commission on Banking and Currency (1933) advocated a stronger federal presence in the banking system, in the form of the Bank of Canada which would have sole right of issue. Incorporated in 1935, it was nationalised in 1938 as the central bank, and acquired a full monopoly on note issue in 1945. From its inception, the Bank of Canada had the power to impose (and change) reserve requirements on the chartered banks. But, since the Bank of Canada also acted as lender-of-last-resort, banks were now able to expand credit in the sure knowledge of being able to acquire the necessary reserves (albeit at a price). The financial system was hastening into the fourth stage of development.

After a long hiatus, new developments in banking structure commenced in 1955 with the merger of two of the smaller Toronto banks, the Bank of Toronto and the Dominion Bank, to form the Toronto-Dominion Bank. This was followed in 1961 by the merger between two other Toronto banks, the Canadian Bank of Commerce and the Imperial Bank of Commerce, with over twenty-four per cent of the market, the second-largest share. Montreal's Royal Bank of Canada had a slightly larger share, and the Bank of Montreal was now pushed down into third place. (See Neufeld 1972, Table 4.6.) Since the 1913 Bank Act, mergers have required the approval of the Minister of Finance.

Meanwhile, the Mercantile Bank of Canada, formed in 1953 in Montreal as a wholly-owned subsidiary of a Dutch bank, came into prominence in 1963 when it was taken over by the First National City Bank of New York and began to encroach on the business of domestic banks. Fearing that this signalled a reversal of the previous trend towards reduced foreign ownership of banks, the government legislated a maximum twenty-five per cent non-resident ownership of banks in 1967. With the growing presence in

Canada of branches of foreign banks in the 1970s, however, a new 'schedule B' category of banks was permitted in the 1980 Bank Act revision which removed the non-resident ownership restriction under certain conditions. By 1986, fifty-six schedule B banks had been established by foreign banks, although their assets only accounted for six per cent of the total for all banks operating in Canada. The Mercantile finally merged with the National Bank of Canada in 1985.

Recent years have seen other entrants to banking by non-bank financial intermediaries. One of the two remaining Quebec Savings Banks was granted a charter in Montreal in 1969 as the Banque Populaire, but it merged with the Banque Provinciale in 1970, as did a new Toronto bank in 1977 (the Unity Bank, chartered in 1972, formed through a subscription). The Banque Provinciale in turn merged with the Banque Canadienne Nationale in 1979, taking the name of the National Bank of Canada. Meanwhile, IAC Ltd. (an acceptance corporation) received a charter in Toronto in 1977 as the Continental Bank.

With Montreal having one of Canada's two primary financial centres, there has always been some consciousness in Quebec of the significance to a regional economy of the location of financial markets. This consciousness was maintained by the struggle between Toronto and Montreal for supremacy, a struggle which Montreal has been losing since the Second World War.

Attempts by the Quebec government to harness some of the development-generating power of finance were first evident in recent years in the design of the Canada and Quebec Pension Plans. Quebec alone among all the provinces chose to administer its own public pension funds. While other provinces may borrow CPP funds for general purposes expenditure, the Quebec Caisse de Depôt et de Placement invests some of its funds in Quebec corporate securities with the stated aim of promoting economic development in the province.

When the separatist movement gathered force in the 1960 and 1970 under the leadership of the Parti Quebecois, emphasis was placed on analysing how the Quebec economy had fared at the hands of national institutions: the federal government financial institutions and corporations with head offices outside Quebec. While Quebec had fared better than the Maritimes, the growing income gap between Quebec and Ontario prompted questions similar to those raised much earlier in the Maritimes about outflows of funds to the rest of Canada coincident with growing financial concentration (although the financial system was by then in its fourth stage, so that the relevant question was now about the location of credit creation rather than the distribution of a given pool of credit).

In 1969 a Government of Quebec Study Committee on Financial Institutions explicitly rejected the federal government's Royal Commission on Banking and Finance (1964) judgement that financial institutions should be as free as possible of public sector influence. Their recommendations led to the establishment of a Quebec deposit insurance agency and Ministry of Financial Institutions. While the Committee admitted the possibility of net outflows of funds through financial institutions, they nevertheless concluded that any attempt to restrict outflows would in itself discourage inflows, possibly worsening the net position. The emphasis of the report was rather on rationalizing the regulatory environment of financial institutions to increase efficiency. Further, since outside competition was seen as an essential ingredient in promoting efficiency, mergers among Quebec institutions were to be encouraged in order to compete more effectively with outside institutions.

Three years later, the Government of Quebec Study Committee on the Securities Industry in Quebec (1972) advocated a more dirigiste approach to strengthening Quebec securities markets. They recommended that the Quebec Securities Commission be given increased powers over securities firms, that outside ownership of securities firms be limited, and that Quebec firms be encouraged to conduct more business in the Quebec market.

Meanwhile, the Parti Quebecois official program in the 1970s contained strong proposals for measures to increase government control over financial flows within Quebec and between the provinces and elsewhere. These proposals included the setting up of a Quebec central bank, a provincial monopoly in such areas as small loans (including consumer credit) and auto insurance, limitations on non-Quebec ownership of financial institutions, and measures to encourage Quebec savers to place their funds with institutions investing primarily in Quebec. The federal government's response included the publication of a series of reports presenting counter-arguments, such as

38

Government of Canada (1978). Once in power, from 1976, the Parti Quebecois government had economic accounts constructed for Quebec. The data were used as evidence that there was a net outflow of funds to the federal government, and also net private sector capital outflows. Meanwhile Statistics Canada had started publishing experimental provincial accounts data, and a prolonged debate ensued as to the relative merits, and possible interpretations, of the respective data sets.[9]

The Quebec government (1979) however modified the strong Parti Quebecois proposals for independent monetary control. The White Paper on sovereignty-association with the rest of Canada proposed rather a unified currency area, but with explicit proportional regional representation on the Board of Directors of the Bank of Canada. The Bank would continue to have jurisdiction over monetary policy and exchange rate policy for Canada and Quebec. But separate additional Canada and Quebec monetary authorities would manage the public debt and handle the government banking business for the two jurisdictions. The Parti Quebecois had concluded that independent currencies and monetary policy for the two areas, given their interdependence, were not feasible. (See Maxwell and Pestieau 1980, chapter three.) No action has yet been taken on these proposals, given the unfavourable outcome of the 1980 referendum on sovereignty-association, and the defeat of the Parti Quebecois government in the 1985 election. Legislation designed to promote French as the province's first language (Bill 101) was however itself instrumental in changing the ownership composition of the financial sector. The decline of Montreal as a financial centre relative to Toronto had already taken the form of (as well as caused) a steady removal of head offices and banks' trading desks since the 1950s; Bill 101 simply accelerated this underlying trend.

The decline of Quebec's financial power focused the attention of Ryba (1974a, 1974b, 1976) on the significance of the location of financial institutions for a region's economic development. While his analysis refers to a period of change in a region's financial structure, it allows insights also into situations of more lasting difference in financial structure between, for example, the Maritimes and Central Canada. Having provided evidence of the shift in financial business from Montreal to Toronto, Ryba (1974a)[10] outlines the types of additional cost arising from this shift, on the basis of interview evidence. Quebec's financial sector incurs the following as a result of operating in a distant market (in Toronto):

(i) carrying costs

(ii)   communications costs

(iii)   information costs

(iv)   exclusion from oligopolistic arrangements

(v)   costs of maintaining a correspondent system.

Quebec's industrial sector, as borrowers and lenders in financial markets incurs these additional costs:

(vi)   remoteness from the major market and thus from market opportunities

(vii)   relative absence of financial sector externalities (research, information etc.)

(viii)   absence of new industry attracted by the presence of the financial centre.

While the interview method is problematic in terms of quantifying the type of cost listed above and the sample base small, the evidence is significant in adding weight to arguments which point to financial structure itself as influencing capital flows and the location of credit creation.

A more detailed and broadly based survey conducted by Ryba and Desnoyers (1975) focused on the question of business finance. The results provide evidence not only of unsatisfied demand for credit among medium-sized business outside Montreal and Quebec City, but also of demand for finance (particularly other than bank credit) which was not even expressed in the market because of lack of information. Large firms, and particularly those in Montreal and Quebec, were found to be sophisticated in their acquisition of credit and allocation of funds, using a wider range of financial instruments both in Quebec and elsewhere. Small and medium sized firms, in contrast, relied primarily on self-financing and on short and medium term chartered bank loans; even with bank loans, the lack of direct contact with bank head-office decision-makers was regarded as an impediment. Medium-sized firms, requiring sizeable capital sums for expansion, were found to be most restricted by limited access to credit facilities as a result of such factors as information barriers, and lack of personal contact with

40

financial intermediaries other than local bank branches. For these firms particularly there was a marked difference between those in Montreal and Quebec City and those elsewhere, the latter using less sophisticated financial instruments, and expressing more dissatisfaction with the financial sector.

This evidence has important implications for the interpretation of 'harder' quantified evidence of business financial experience. Survey evidence is sometimes dismissed on the grounds that it records respondants' accounts of their own behaviour rather than the behaviour itself. Both this survey, however, and Ryba (1974a), demonstrate the importance of lack of expertise and information on the part of borrowers and lenders outside financial centres. Evidence of rejected applications for bank credit, for example, is incomplete as a measure of unsatisfied demand if some businesses do not make applications through lack of knowledge or else because they strongly anticipate rejection. Of the forty-three per cent surveyed businesses which used self-financing for over half their financing needs, fifty-three per cent gave as the reason that it was 'easier' than using other sources. This heavy reliance on self-financing is an inhibiting factor in terms of economic development, since savings must be accumulated before investment can occur; bank credit, rather, promotes more rapid expansion by allowing investment to anticipate saving.

Ryba (1974a) advocated the establishment of a Quebec International Financial Centre as a galvaniser of a strengthened financial sector; it would act as an information and research centre, a centralised money and bond market and a promoter of connections with foreign money and bond markets. In addition he proposes a change in Bank of Canada philosophy and practice towards active participation in regional financial markets. The purpose of these recommendations is to increase the retention of Quebec savings, attract savings from elsewhere (particularly other countries) and to improve the process of intermediation between savers and investors. The analysis is thus set in the context of a fixed pool of available credit, i.e. the third stage of banking development, which has not obtained in Canada since the 1930s.

The net flow of saving into or out of Quebec was not the main concern of the Government of Quebec Study Group on Saving (1980), but the implicit view of the financial system is equally outdated. They were concerned more

41

with the structure of saving and the form in which it is made available to Quebec borrowers. The Group's recommendations are designed to increase the efficiency of the Quebec financial system with two ends in view. First this would increase the availability of funds to local borrowers by channelling intermediation through Quebec institutions, and thus avoiding the cultural barriers involved in intermediation through non-Quebec institutions. Second, even if the amount of funds available were unchanged, a greater degree of self-determination would result.

Efficiency is to be promoted by increased competition. It is recommended that the povincial government liberalise its regulation of local financial institutions, allowing them to compete with the banks in the provision of short-term business credit, for example. The ability of these institutions to compete on new ground would be promoted by deposit insurance to maintain depositors' confidence. In general, government intervention is recommended only in cases of persistent credit gaps and then in a form designed to encourage private institutions to reduce those gaps.

The recommendations accord in spirit with those of the earlier studies discussed above: government intervention is required to restore the Quebec financial sector to its former strength (including the range of local institutions existing before bank concentration gathered force) but government is then to allow the market to determine the allocation of credit. Freedom of capital flows within Quebec and from outside is to be encouraged. It is curious that financial relationships outside Canada should not be analyzed in the same way as those with Toronto. The widespread assumption is that, if only the loss of financial business from Montreal to Toronto could be reversed, market forces within financial markets would act in the best interests of Quebec. This response to financial developments differs markedly from that of the Western provinces, which have never experienced local financial sovereignty.

3.2.3 The Prairie Region and British Columbia

The legislation of 1870-1 extended to the banks the facility of lending against security of goods in warehouses or in transit. This greatly increased their ability to finance the movement of what was to become the major staple:

wheat. The wheat producing Prairie provinces, Manitoba, Saskatchewan, and Alberta, as well as British Columbia, were settled relatively late in the period of Canada's banking development, and thus banking needs tended to be met more by branches of existing banks (predominantly headquartered in Ontario and Quebec) than the chartering of new ones. Only eight of the new Western banks chartered around the turn of the century employed their charters (thirteen remained unused). Branches of central Canadian banks had already opened in the West by then, and all the local banks were taken over by 1931. These banks were preceded by the establishment of some highly successful private banks, notably Alloway and Campion in Winnipeg (taken over by the Bank of Commerce) which specialised in foreign exchange business, dealing with immigrants' transactions, and Macdonald's Bank in Victoria (closed due to robbery) which specialised in gold-rush-related transactions.

In the early days of western Canada's economic development, therefore, large capital inflows were effected through the intermediation of financial institutions in Toronto and Montreal, meaning, effectively, that banking started off at stage three. Most of the capital was directed towards railroad development and wheat traders. As far as individual farmers were concerned, financing was either inadequate or presented on unfavourable terms. The sentiment behind proposals for monetary reform was thus populist, echoing the sentiment among farmers in the Mid-west of the United States.

The banks were free to make short-term secured loans to farmers, but not conventional mortgage loans before 1967. This restriction was supported by the banks, who only started petitioning for a change in legislation on mortgage lending in 1962 (see Neufeld 1972, p.111). Farm purchases were thus financed by own savings, or borrowing from mortgage loan companies, trust companies, insurance companies, or, often, individual lenders (see Mackintosh 1935). Only after 1913 could harvested grain be used as security for short-term bank loans. The three-month term of these loans did not suit farmers whose production cycle is twelve-months, so they were frequently forced to sell grain in order to repay loans, whether the market price was favourable or not.

Bank credit continued to be made available more freely to traders in wheat, who had always been able to borrow on security of grain in warehouses or in

43

transit. Indeed, the original intention of allowing banks to make loans secured by commodities at all was 'to provide assistance to wholesale manufacturers and wholesale purchasers of and dealers in primary products' (Jamieson 1953, p.45). That Prairie farmers felt a need which was not being met by the existing financial intstitutions is evidenced by two attempts in the early 1900s to obtain charters for agricultural banks; both attempts failed.

By the Great Depression, Prairie farmers were heavily in debt, not least because of the disadvantaged market position forced on them by the inflexibility of the financial system. Three-quarters of the debt was mortgaged on property. Of the short-term debt, around one-third was due to chartered banks. McIvor (1958, pp.148-9) thus estimates that the banks only accounted for around eight per cent of farm debt at the time; the bulk was held by individual lenders. By 1931 almost half the average farmer's income was required to service this debt (see McIvor 1958, p. 148). Saskatchewan was worst hit, with a fall in farm income of seventy-two per cent from 1928-9 to 1933, compared to an average of 48% for Canada as a whole. Representatives of Western agriculture lobbied the federal government early in the Depression for money-financed public works together with an exchange depreciation, which would boost grain prices relative to farm costs. But, according to the Report of the Royal Commission on Dominion-Provincial Relations (1940, Book I, p.152), 'Canada ... should do nothing to weaken the confidence of either the internal or foreign investor'.

Bankers in general appear to have been oblivious to the special credit needs of agricultural producers, whose income fluctuates significantly both within and between years. The following is an expression of the views of a banker who had experience of the west:

> the trouble ... is not with the system, but is due to deficiencies of administration of what is recognized by financial critics as one of the best banking systems in the world - deficiencies most of which are incidental to a period of rapid agricultural development and therefore scarcely avoidable ... How could it be successfully argued that a banking system which has so admirably served the [farmers of the old-settled Provinces] is inadequate for the requirements of the Western Provinces? (Brown 1918-9, pp.267-8)

The severity of the debt burden, not only on farmers but also on the provincial governments during the Depression, was instrumental in focusing populist attention on the rôle of the banks in the Western economy. Of the two major populist movements which emerged in the 1930s, the Co-operative Commonwealth Federation identified finance as one of a range of sources of the Prairies' economic problems, while the Social Credit League identified it as the sole source.

The Regina Manifesto which spelled out the CCF programme in 1933 specified the 'socialization of finance' as a necessary adjunct to economic planning. Chartered banks were to be taken over by the state, as were insurance companies, 'one of the main channels for the investment of individual savings' (Cooperative Commonwealth Federation, 1933, p.2). The thinking behind the Manifesto was elaborated by the League for Social Reconstruction (1935). The banks' significance stemmed from their ability to control the allocation of credit for different purposes, on the one hand, and to influence the cyclical pattern of general economic conditions, on the other. Since banks expand credit where high returns are expected, they fuel expansions. Retrenchment of credit when speculative bubbles burst brings about a cumulative contraction. The purpose of nationalising the banking system was 'to finance depressed regions or industries or re-housing plans, etc. by curtailing the financing of luxury trades, stock market speculation and the rest' (League for Social Reconstruction, 1935, p.304). It is significant that the behaviour of bankers was accepted as rational according to the profit motive of institutions operating in isolation. The passage quoted above continues as follows: 'But it will not be done voluntarily by private profit-making institutions - nor is there any reason why we should expect it'. Similarly, 'If they do not lend already, the reason is that such loans are not liquid, or not profitable' (League for Social Reconstruction, 1935, p.303). The purpose of the Manifesto was to promote collective well-being, which inevitably conflicts with the well-being of individual institutions which happen to hold economic power.

In contrast, the Social Credit League identified the prevailing system of finance as the sole source of economic problems, and in so doing attacked the actions of individual bankers. In the words of their mentor Major Douglas

45

(who was much less vituperative than many of his followers):

> It must, unfortunately, be recognised that the Eastern financial interests, acting through the Dominion Cabinet and otherwise, are implacably opposed to any effective action which would divest them to the slightest extent of the tremendous power they have achieved by their monopoly of financial credit. ... I believe that these interests are capable of sacrificing the population of Alberta to any extent which may be necessary to maintain their power, and are, either from lack of imagination, or from less excusable causes, insensible to the suffering which may be involved.
> (Douglas 1937, pp.91-2)

According to Social Credit theory, the importance of finance stems from the necessity of credit in maintaining the level of aggregate demand. Douglas, influenced by Hobson's underconsumption theory, argued that firms' costs could be classified as payments to individuals ('A payments') in the form of wages, dividends, etc. and payments to institutions ('B payments') for raw materials, bank charges, etc. A payments are used for expenditure, but B payments disappear from the expenditure stream in payments to banks as repayment of loans, bank charges or interest payments. Any savings out of A payments constitute an additional drain on the flow of spending. Of the total cost of output, (A+B), only A at most would be returned as sales revenue unless additional credit were made available by the banks. Unemployment, then, is the result of credit expansion which is too small to raise expenditure to the value (A+B). While it was pointed out that B payments for raw materials, intermediate goods, etc. would, in part at least, become A payments to employees in those industries, Douglas rested his case on the sequencing of production, with credit being necessary in advance to finance production. Douglas' analysis of the financial system as such was not, however, very profound: 'The financial system is essentially a system of black magic, and one of the best protections against black magic is not to believe in it'. (Douglas 1937, p.95)

Douglas' proposed monetary reforms for Alberta involved shifting to the government the responsibility for extending credit in the province (with transitional refinancing of the government's own debt which was at that time very burdensome). The distribution of credit was to be effected by a national dividend paid to all residents, to consumers to increase demand relative to the costs of production (A+B) and to producers to allow them to reduce prices relative to the costs of production. Aberhart's government, however, diverged from Douglas' proposals. First, he proposed a national dividend of twenty-five dollars a month, payable to every adult citizen in Alberta, and financed by a sales tax. Tax increases were also introduced to reduce the government's borrowing requirement. In both cases, Douglas' argument that taxation, as a withdrawal from the expenditure stream, simply aggravated the shortage of credit, was ignored.

In addition, Aberhart was influenced by the theories of Silvio Gesell (against Douglas' advice) to introduce taxed currency with the purpose of speeding up the velocity of circulation, and thus increasing expenditure. Notes called Alberta prosperity certificates bore a tax of two per cent (later reduced to one per cent) per week (payable by affixing a two per cent stamp to the note) and expired after two years. Rather than inducing larger and more frequent expenditures, these notes were exchanged quickly for other forms of money. They were put into circulation through government payments of wages and welfare, but in its enthusiasm for keeping them in circulation the government would not accept them in payment of taxes. The scheme folded within six months. In fact all Aberhart's financial reform legislation was overturned by the Supreme Court of Canada in 1937.

When the CCF gained power in Saskatchewan in 1944 it did not attempt to implement the Regina Manifesto, as far as financial institutions were concerned; the nationalisation of banks had been pledged as a national, rather than provincial policy. The New Democratic Party was formed in 1961 as the result of an alliance between the CCF, the Canadian Labor Congress and other groups. Within the NDP, the original aims of the Regina Manifesto were revitalised by the Waffle Group's Manifesto in 1969 but sank from prominence with the group's demise in 1973.

Some limited financial reform was attempted by the provincial NDP governments in Manitoba and BC. The Government of Manitoba (1973) set itself guidelines for financial reforms which were viewed as feasible for one province within a national financial system. On the one hand, the guidelines pointed to a lack of competition in banking in Manitoba, causing the costs of financial services to be excessive, and on the other to a massive outflow of funds effected by the banks, trust companies and insurance companies. The proposals for reform were the setting up of provincial Treasury branches to increase competition and reduce costs of services, and the strengthening of credit unions. The credit unions however argued that they, along with the new Northland Bank of Calgary, had already expanded to fill the gap which Treasury branches might have filled and that they were the appropriate vehicle for channelling services and credit to additional areas and sectors. No action was taken on Treasury branches, and the Government concentrated instead on its relationship with the credit unions.

Meanwhile, in British Columbia, the Social Credit government had been petitioning the federal government since 1964 to allow government equity in banks.[11] The rationale was that financial needs in BC would be better met by a bank whose head office was in BC than Central Canada; government equity participation was designed as encouragement to a new local private sector bank, rather than as a vehicle for controlling financial flows. However, government participation in banks was precluded by the 1967 Bank Act, and the Bank of British Columbia was established as a purely private bank in 1968.[12] The issue re-emerged in 1975 when the New Democratic government introduced enabling legislation for the establishment of the British Columbia Savings and Trust Corporation, an institution to perform banking, trust and insurance functions. The credit unions were invited to purchase ten per cent of the authorised shares. In contrast to the previous government's motivation, the NDP government explained its entry into banking in terms of competing with existing institutions, particularly the banks, and as an attempt to retain funds in the province to promote economic development. The 1975 provincial election prevented action being taken on the corporation.

The issue of the competitiveness of the existing banking system and the net flow of funds out of Western Canada into Central Canada had already been thrashed out at the Western Economic Opportunities Conference (in Calgary in 1973) called by the federal government with the four Western provinces. The provinces' position paper criticised the oligopolistic structure of the banking system and its Central Canadian orientation. The policies of the federal government, it was argued, had promoted a concentration of financial and industrial resources which 'worked against the allocation of financial and production resources to bring balance to the economies of all regions of Canada' (Premiers of Manitoba, Alberta, Saskatachewan and British Columbia, 1973, p.3). The banking system was charged with being unresponsive to the financial needs of Western Canada; the diversification of the Western economy required 'an adequate availability of financial resources at competitive rates through institutions which are responsive to the particular needs of the Western Provinces' (*ibid.*).

The Canadian Bankers' Association response (Canadian Bankers' Association, 1974) was, on the one hand, to argue that banks did respond to regional needs at competitive rates and, on the other, to provide evidence that there was a *net inflow* of funds to the Western provices through the banking system. From that time, regional banking data have been published on a quarterly basis. (They are discussed in some detail in Chapter four.) The federal government addressed the question of the competitiveness of the banking system (Government of Canada, 1973). On the grounds that the banking system is 'highly competitive', the position paper argued that any attempt to regulate banking practice further would lead to a misallocation of resources and increased credit costs. In other words, if there *was* a net outflow of funds from any region, it was the result of a competitive financial market allocating resources efficiently. At the same time, it was admitted that the concentration of head offices in Toronto and Montreal together with the 'interlocking nature of the corporate business community, results in a lack of responsiveness to the needs for development capital in the West' (*ibid.*). Federal government willingness to contemplate limited provincial government participation in new banks, announced at the 1973 Conference, eventually bore fruit in the 1980 Bank Act.

Another theme to re-emerge in the Western provinces in recent years is the Social Credit national dividend policy. Both Alberta and Saskatchewan set up Heritage Savings and Trust Funds with revenue from oil and gas production, to act as a pool of funds for diversifying the provincial economies to provide for stable incomes in the future. In Alberta, a distribution of funds to residents started in 1982 in the form of mortgage relief. Indeed there has been some discussion as to whether the future strength of the economy might be promoted

49

more effectively by distributing resource revenues to residents by a national dividend rather than administering them within the public sector (see McMillan and Norrie 1980). In 1982 and 1983, however, falling gas and oil production and prices took their toll on general revenues, so that money was diverted from the Fund to finance government expenditure. In Saskatchewan, the Heritage Fund was used primarily to fund operations of Crown Corporations, social and economic development projects, and resource conservation and development projects.

The main feature of banking developments in the Prairie provinces in recent years has been the shift westward of the economic axis, particularly with the expansion of oil and gas wealth. In 1968 the Bank of British Columbia was chartered in Vancouver. Expressions of interest in promoting, and having a twenty per cent ownership of, such a bank by the BC government in 1964 had encouraged the federal government to include in the 1967 Bank Act a prohibition on ownership of voting shares of existing banks by any shareholder in excess of ten per cent of the total, and of any voting shares by provincial governments. (The 1980 Bank Act revision allowed for a twenty five per cent maximum government holding of voting shares of new banks only, to be reduced to a maximum of twenty per cent after ten years.) Four other new banks opened in the west: in 1975 the Northland Bank set up by Western credit union and cooperative leaders and the Canadian Commercial Bank were set up in Alberta, the Western and Pacific Bank of Canada in British Columbia in 1984, and the Bank of Alberta in 1984.

However, by 1985, falling raw material prices (particularly those for oil and gas) had seriously eroded the economic advantage enjoyed by the Western provinces in the 1970s. As a result of bad loans, both the Northland Bank and the Canadian Commercial Bank experienced such severe liquidity problems that they were forced to go into liquidation. The Bank of British Columbia also experienced difficulties but managed to survive another year. But in December 1986 it was finally taken over by a schedule B bank (a wholly owned subsidiary of the Hong Kong and Shanghai Banking Corporation). Although most other banks were also affected by defaults, their greater portfolio diversification and/or their greater ability to inspire confidence among suppliers of funds (depositors and other financial institutions) allowed

50

them to weather the storm. There is indeed some question as to whether the liquidation of the Canadian Commercial Bank was warranted other than by a self-fulfilling erosion of confidence which discouraged depositors and other lenders. At any rate, the process of disposing of loans (the liabilities predominantly of Prairie businesses) was generally expected to have adverse ripple effects on these businesses and the Prairie economy in general. By the end of 1986, the two remaining western banks accounted for well under one per cent of the total assets of Schedule A banks.

3.3 SAVINGS BANKS, CREDIT UNIONS AND CAISSES POPULAIRES

While the chartered banks dealt primarily with traders and upper and middle income depositors, the savings banks provided savings facilities for lower income groups, and were often run by trustees with a view to encouraging thrift. The first was the Montreal District Savings Bank, formed in 1819. As with many private savings banks, it was closely associated with a chartered bank (the Bank of Montreal) and was eventually absorbed by it. While savings banking was encouraged by provincial legislation, the management of savings banks was not in general successful. The 1840s saw an array of new savings banks in Ontario and Quebec, but loans were often made without adequate security and the volunteer management was inadequate to the task of managing larger deposits and the array of local (particularly public) securities in which they could invest. By 1871, savings banks were required to obtain charters and operate as limited liability, joint-stock corporations. Only two Quebec banks accepted this change, one of which, the Montreal City and District Savings Bank, still functions today under federal legislation. After 1948, they were permitted to make mortgage loans and some unsecured loans to individuals and businesses.

The difficulties associated with trustee management encouraged the provincial governments in the Maritime provinces to set up their own savings banks: in the 1830s in Nova Scotia and Newfoundland, in the 1840s in New Brunswick, and in the 1860s in Prince Edward Island. This proved to be a more simple means of regulating the management of savings deposits and the channelling of funds to the public sector. These banks were all taken over by the federal government at Confederation in 1867 to form a federal government savings bank, which gathered funds to finance railroad construction in the West. It was later absorbed into the Post Office Savings Bank, which in turn was dissolved in 1968. Ontario and Manitoba also set up Savings Offices in 1920, with the express purpose of gathering funds to distribute as agricultural credit. Manitoba's offices closed in 1930; the Ontario offices still do business, although deposits are channelled directly into general revenues. In contrast, Alberta's Treasury Branches, started in 1938, continue to make a wide range of loans and offer a wide range of deposit services.

The savings banks suffered an erosion of their market in the 1880s at the hands of the chartered banks. With the lucrative right of note issue passing to the federal government and demand for notes being relatively stagnant, the banks were turning to savings deposits as an alternative source of business. Between 1875 and 1905, the banks increased their savings deposits from 15.9% to 44.2% of total liabilities. (See Naylor 1975,p.87.) Because banks devoted assets to discounting trade bills rather more than public sector securities, this development resulted in a redirection of funds.

The non-bank sector in Quebec responded by setting up co-operative savings institutions called caisses populaires from 1900. Similar institutions called credit unions were started in 1920 in Nova Scotia and in Ontario, with a subsequent strong development in the Prairies. Both have a hierarchical structure, with centrals supervising operations and clearing payments. The caisses populaires' main stated purpose is, like the savings banks, to encourage thrift; they traditionally have lent only around half their assets to members (mostly in the form of residential mortgages). The credit unions on the other hand were an outgrowth of the Reformist movement, filling a gap left by the private banks, with the aim of improving credit facilities. Up to 80% of assets are lent to members, as mortgage or consumer loans.

3.4 MORTGAGE LOAN COMPANIES AND TRUST COMPANIES

Mortgage loans, which the banks were not permitted to make, were initially the main preserve of mortgage loan companies and trust companies. The first mortgage loan companies were formed in the 1840s as building societies which terminated when all members' homes had been built. Most companies were incorporated in Central Canada, initially funding farm mortgages there. Operations were extended to Manitoba and further West as the wheat economy grew in the 1880s. Farm mortgages were generally given for an initial five-year period, which left borrowers dependent on refinancing at whatever terms were made available thereafter. Rates were consistently higher in the Prairies than in Ontario. Having been authorized since 1874 to raise funds by debenture issues, the mortgage loan companies were able to bring funds in from British investors who were attracted by the boom conditions in Western Canada. (One Quebec company was given monopoly access to the French market.) In the 1890s, as grain prices weakened, the mortgage companies turned their attention back to Ontario and Quebec where the rapid expansion of the cities called for new mortgage funding.

Trust companies did not come on the scene in significant numbers until somewhat later than mortgage loan companies, although the first one, the Trust and Loan Company of Canada, was formed in Kingston in 1843. The primary function of trust companies is to administer trusts and thus depends on the accumulation of large estates. However, they can also issue claims on their own behalf and make loans on their own behalf (assets mainly consisting of mortgage loans but also purchases of stocks and bonds). The first trust company raised funds mainly in the London market. Subsequent trust companies, formed around the turn of the century, were each closely associated, through interlocking directorships, with the chartered banks. All were located in Central Canada except for one in Halifax and one in Vancouver, and of the former, four companies were dominant. Legislation just after the turn of the century empowered trust companies effectively to take deposits and thus (short of issuing cheques) perform banking funtions. When, in the 1960s, the six per cent ceiling on bank loans limited the degree to which banks could attract deposits and the trust companies started offering chequing deposits, the latter's share of total deposits grew impressively. This trend was inhibited in 1967 when the six per cent ceiling was lifted and banks were given more general access to conventional mortgage lending. While the public sector issued or approved over half of outstanding mortgages in the 1950s, the proportion had fallen to one-third by 1980. (See Economic Council of Canada, 1982b, p.69.)

3.5 SALES FINANCE AND CONSUMER LOAN COMPANIES

While trust companies, along with the banks, credit unions anad caisses populaires all extend consumer credit, it is the sales finance and consumer loan companies which specialise in this area. The former provide credit, to be paid off in instalments, along with a particular purchase; the latter provide credit (also sometimes on an instalment basis) to finance consumption in general. Consumer credit had always been available in some form in Canada, often provided by retailers. But it was the expansion of the automobile market in the early 1900s which encouraged the emergence of the first sales finance companies. There followed a proliferation of organisations providing consumer credit, many being attached to particular manufacturing corporations (such as General Motors). Also, because many of these corporations were American, and since sales finance had emerged earlier south of the border, sales finance in Canada had a large American component. (See Neufeld 1972, pp.334-6.)

The first companies were incorporated in Ontario and Manitoba in 1920. After 1957, at a time of increasing consumer borrowing, sales finance companies lost much of their market share to the chartered banks; this reflected partly a shift in preference towards general consumer loans rather than purchase-specific loans. (The consumer loan companies, many being subsidiaries of sales finance companies and specializing in general consumer loans, retained their small share of the market.) While until the early 1950s the sales finance companies had relied on bank borrowing for over trwenty per cent of their funds, reliance shifted thereafter to issues of short and long-term notes. Access to the money market was soured somewhat by the failure of two Canadian companies in 1965 and 1966.

3.6 INSURANCE COMPANIES, PENSION FUNDS, MUTUAL FUNDS AND INVESTMENT COMPANIES

Since the chartered banks restricted their lending primarily to the short-term, business had to turn to alternative sources of long-term financing. The major domestic sources of such funds are insurance companies, pension funds, mutual funds and investment companies.

Insurance companies have grown to take second place to the banks in terms of share of total financial assets. The first Canadian fire insurance company was formed in Halifax as early as 1809, and the first in Upper Canada in 1833. The Canada Life Assurance Company, formed in Hamilton in 1847, was the first life insurance company. Because life insurance was used as a vehicle for savings, the business has grown much more rapidly than fire and casualty insurance. In 1869, life insurance companies accounted for thirty-eight per cent of the insurance sector, and eighty-one per cent in 1969. (See Neufeld 1972, Appendix Table B.)

All types of insurance were originally dominated by British and American companies. But evidence of malpractice, poor management and failure of insurance companies prompted the passing of legislation in 1875 and 1877 providing for supervision and regulation of assets. Companies were required to hold sufficient Canadian assets to cover their Canadian liabilities; non-Canadian companies had to lodge title to those assets with the Minister of Finance or an approved trust company. As a result many of the British and American companies withdrew from the market, leaving the field open to the Canadian companies, which in turn later extended their business overseas. Further restrictive legislation passed in 1919 drove out of business most of the 'friendly societies' which had been meeting insurance needs in small communities. Most head offices are located in Central Canada, the major exception being the Great West Life Company in Winnipeg. Although the life insurance market is dominated by one company, Sun Life, there is a large number of smaller companies, since legislation has discouraged mergers. In 1978 Sun Life moved its head office from Montreal to Toronto.

Because the liabilities of life insurance companies are actuarially predictable (unlike bank liabilities, for example) they have been free to invest in long term securities. They are thus major purchasers of corporation bonds and stocks; other major asset categories are mortgage loans and government bonds. Fire and casualty insurance companies' asset structure is similar, but with a higher proportion of liquid assets. Automobile insurance, the major category of casualty insurance, has come under the public sector in Saskatchewan (in 1945) and in the 1970s in Manitoba, British Columbia, and to a lower minimum level of insurance in Quebec.

As a vehicle for life-time savings, the pension plans have been a major source of competition for insurance companies in recent years. Private plans' assets by 1970 had reached seventy per cent of life insurance company assets. Initially, only the federal government offered pension annuities (from 1898), and in 1919 introduced special tax treatment for particular pension contributions and benefits. Universal pensions were introduced in 1927, subject to a means test which was removed in 1951. The Canada Pension Plan (CPP) was set up in 1965, and Quebec took the option of setting up its own plan, the Quebec Pension Plan (QPP). Each other province can borrow CPP funds in proportion to the contributions made by its residents; any of the province's share not used thus is invested in federal securities. The QPP is free to invest in private sector securities, and uses its funds as a positive vehicle for supporting local enterprise. Private pension plans did not emerge until 1939. (1938 legislation permitted tax deductability of employers' pension contributions.) Like life insurance companies, they are free to invest in long-term securities. Pension plans are major purchasers of provincial bonds and corporate stocks and bonds.

Individual investors in corporate securities achieve some protection from risk by channelling their money through mutual funds and investment companies; these companies pool individals' funds to spread their risks in the stock market. Mutual fund shares are redeemable by the fund at their net asset value while ivestment company shares can only be sold on the market. Mutual fund companies are thus called open-end companies, and investment companies called closed-end companies.

Canada's first investment company was formed in Toronto in 1901, filling a gap in the securities market which other institutions were unwilling, or forbidden by legislation, to fill. Additional companies were formed in the

56

1920s funded partially by foreign capital. The first Canadian mutual fund was formed in 1932. Many investment companies failed in 1929. Most growth after the 1940s was experienced by the mutual funds. But in recent years this growth has been inhibited by the trust companies and banks moving into this field. Although some investment companies have owned a controlling interest in companies whose shares they held, only two major holding companies have emerged in Canada: Power Corporation (formed in 1925) and Argus Corporation (1945).

Finally, the public sector has also been a source of long-term funds for both industry and agriculture, the major federal agencies being the Industrial Development Bank and the Farm Credit Corporation, respectively. Provincial agencies have administered credit schemes for farmers since the 1870s (in Ontario) but more particularly in the inter-war period. Agencies designed specifically to provide, or guarantee, industrial loans were not formed until the 1950s and 1960s. Both Alberta and Saskatchewan set up Heritage Savings and Trust Funds in 1976 and 1978 respectively, with a portion of natural resource revenues; their aim was to finance diversification of their economies to reduce dependence on oil and gas. While the other federal and provincial credit agencies account for a very small proportion of total financial assets, these two Funds are amassing very sizeable assets. (See Donner 1982, chapter six.) At the end of March 1982, the Alberta Heritage Fund's assets stood at eleven billion dollars and Saskatchewan's at just under one bilion dollars, or over three per cent of those of the chartered banks, between the two funds.

3.7 FOREIGN INFLUENCES ON THE DEVELOPMENT OF THE FINANCIAL SYSTEM

The development of Canadian financial institutions was strongly influenced by external factors. In this section we discuss first the external influences on ideas about institutional arrangements in Canada and second the more direct influence of the need to import foreign capital, to allow credit creation to grow in line with demand.

Canada has always been an open economy, not only in the sense of having a high proportion of activity devoted to international trade, but also in the sense of having a large proportion of financial flows international rather than domestic. This, together with the influence of the colonial authorities on banking legislation, has added up to a strong external influence on Canada's financial system and its regional components.

Developments in Canadian banking legislation, described in the second section, were strongly influenced by concerns which were current in the British banking system. (See Hammond 1957, pp.632-701.) The greater emphasis on the liquidity of bank assets following the 1836-9 crisis, and the proposals made in the 1840s concerning the limitation of the banks' note issue and the introduction of a Dominion note issue were influenced by a parallel move towards greater caution in the British banking system. British legislation of 1844 and 1845 required that additions to the note issue be backed by gold reserves, control being centralised in one bank, the Bank of England. This legislation was opposed (unsuccessfully) particularly by the Scottish bankers whose institutional structure closely resembled that in Canada at that time. They argued that individual bankers, with their knowledge of local trade and traders, were the best judges of credit requirements. The Canadian bankers, putting forward the same arguments, succeeded in postponing control of their note issue until 1870, and the emergence of a bank under federal government control until 1935. Nevertheless these restrictive influences on the Canadian banking system at what was still an early stage in its development probably had an adverse influence on Canada's economic development (in the sense of a broad-based expansion of industry in the manufacturing sector, as opposed to staples and trade).

There is some debate as to how stable Canada's banking system was in the nineteenth century. On the one hand, Easterbrook and Aitken (1956, p.455) reflect probably the majority view that the chartered banks' stability is demonstrated by an absence of failures during the 1836-9 crisis. On the other hand, Naylor (1975, chapter four) points to the high incidence of bank failures at other times as evidence of instability. The view is universally held, however, that Canadian bankers were very conservative in their asset management, a conservatism reinforced by the emphasis on asset liquidity after 1839 and the later controls on the note issue. Caution, as the vehicle for banking stability, was the reason given for discouraging the proliferation of new banks and for limiting credit to other sectors than trade. In contrast, the private banks with their higher failure rate provided for a wide range of financial needs. While some unsuccessful projects, or poor crops, meant defaults on loans, eventually discouraging depositors and thus enforcing closure of private banks, the fact remains that many successful farms and businesses had in the meantime been provided with the necessary seed capital by the private banks.

When the Scottish banking system came under strict Bank of England control in 1845, it had already enjoyed a century and a half of relative freedom, during which time bank failures were frequent but strong economic growth was financed. Thereafter the Scottish banks consolidated their position and became distinctly more cautious. In Canada, caution was dominant at a much earlier stage in the development of the chartered banking system, leaving it to other institutions, domestic and external, to finance industry and agriculture in their early stages of development.

External influences were also evident among those who argued for changes in the banking system towards a larger number of local banks with much more broadly-based portfolios. Banking in the United States provided a convenient example of how this could be effected. While the early Canadian charters were modelled on the First Bank of the United States, this had in turn been modelled on the Bank of England, with the facility of branching. But the First Bank's success in exerting influence on the United States financial system and on its government aroused the hostility of the anti-trust movement and the agrarian movement and its charter was not renewed. The success of this lobby in promoting a unit banking system in the United States (a system of no branching or branching only within a restricted area) fuelled a similar reformist movement in Canada. Easterbrook and Aitken (1956, p.452) contend however that, in contrast to the United States, Canada's agricultural sector did not come to prominence early enough to influence the banking structure. Thus the timing of Canada's settlement and development, relative to the establishment of banking practices, seems to have been crucial in determining the future influence of the financial system on regional development.

59

External influences were perhaps most keenly felt in terms of the provision of much-needed capital. As a developing country in the nineteenth and early twentieth centuries, Canada required capital inflows not only to finance new industry but also to supply foreign exchange. Hard currency was required to pay for the imports of manufactured goods of value in excess of exports, and before the development of the banking system, for domestic circulation. Britain was the dominant supplier of capital until the First World War, after which the United States became the dominant supplier.

Most domestic capital which was not employed directly to self-finance investment was initially tied up in the Canadian banks. Since the dominant banking institutions, the chartered banks, concentrated their assets in short-term mercantile credit, financing for industrial or infrastructure projects was largely dependent on external capital. The main intermediaries in the development of a market in Canadian securities up to Confederation were the private London banking houses of Baring Brothers and Glyn's. A notable feature of these bond issues was strong government involvement, particularly for the financing of projects in infrastructure development. In spite of government involvement, some of the early projects, notably the Welland Canal in the 1830s and the Grand Trunk railroad in the 1850s, ran into severe financial difficulties, souring the London market for Canadian securities. Many subsequent political and policy developments can be explained in terms of attempts to appease the foreign investor. (See Naylor 1975, chapters two and seven.)

By 1896, Canadian borrowing was dominated by federal and provincial bond issues and those for government-backed projects. By then the federal government had two further major sources of revenue to finance projects, in particular the construction of the Canadian Pacific Railway: tariff revenue on imported manufactured goods, and deposits in the federal savings bank. But the chartered bank entry into the savings deposit business eroded much of that revenue source (as it did for provincial governments operating savings banks) and forced governments to make further sorties into the London capital market. Provincial governments were particularly dependent on foreign capital since their revenue base had been greatly eroded as a result of Confederation. The federal government therefore involved itself in provincial decision-making in order to protect Canada's general credit position in London.

Between 1896 and 1910 the breakdown of public bond issues in London by sector was as follows: railways 42%, federal and provincial governments 24%, municipal governments 9%, utilities 5%, mining 2%, and miscellaneous (including industrial) 18%. (See Naylor 1975, p.231.) Thirteen percentage points of the miscellaneous total were due to bond issues between 1909 and 1910; it was only after 1908 that British funds flowed into industrial bonds, financing widespread mergers.

Capital inflows have continued since then to be a major factor in the financing of major projects, particularly in the field of natural resources exploitation. At the same time, domestic wealth has increased to such an extent that Easterbrook and Aitken claimed in 1956 that Canada was capital self-sufficient, outward flows being of a similar magnitude to inward flows. Since then, however, oil and gas projects in particular have increased capital requirements and capital inflows have generally exceeded capital outflows. The provincial governments have looked increasingly to overseas markets (New York, London and further afield) for bond financing. The major exception is the domestic borrowing facility made available by the Alberta Heritage Fund to other provinces on equal market terms. Alberta itself has never borrowed money on the bond market since 1936, when its debt was so overextended that default was necessary. In foreign markets, the provinces have different bond ratings which correspond to the underwriters' perceptions of their economic and financial stability. The ability of poorer provinces to float bonds has been aided by the federal government's Fiscal Stabilization Program which provides for federal payments to any province whose revenue drops in absolute terms from one year to the next due to an economic downturn. (This guarantee is now qualified with respect to a drop due to a fall in natural resource revenues.)

3.8 FISCAL FEDERALISM

While we are concerned here primarily with financial markets as such, the need for finance and the capacity to generate it within different regions is influenced also by financial flows arising from federal-provincial fiscal arrangements. In this section we consider briefly the factors underlying fiscal flows of funds.

The current elaborate system of federal-provincial fiscal transfers dates from the 1950s when the federal government took over personal and corporate income taxing powers from the provinces in exchange for a system of transfers to ensure that a minimum standard of social services was provided across the country. But the establishment of the federal (then called Dominion) government at Confederation had fiscal implications of more immediate interest as far as provision of finance for investment is concerned. According to the Rowell-Sirois Report of 1940 which underpinned post-World War II fiscal arrangements:

> The largest single item of public expenditure in the colonies had been the promotion of economic development. One of the major purposes of Confederation was to apply still greater energies to this task and to provide still larger financial resources for the purpose. In effect, the Dominion was a great holding company designed to unify the efforts of the colonies in realising the opportunities of a transcontinental domain. All the provincial assets which could be adapted to that purpose were transferred to the Dominion as were the debts which the provinces had incurred in acquiring them. (Smiley, ed., 1963, p.56).

In the face of financial constraints on economic development, then, the state undertook a key role which was to be characteristic of Canadian economic history, raising finance and distributing it according to the government's development objectives. The state was less constrained in its ability to create credit and distribute it at will, than were private sector financial institutions, although ultimately it was dependent on the goodwill of foreign investors. Investment finance from this source, then, was dependent on the perceptions in other countries (particularly Britain and the United States) of the potential of the Canadian economy. Meanwhile, the jurisdiction of the federal government over regional economic development continues to be a matter for debate, with provinces objecting to the centralisation of development strategy.

The federal government's financial contributions to social service expenditure (now under a system of block grants) contributes to a more even pattern of regional development across regions, to the extent that these social services provide infrastructure support to local industry and to the extent that provincial revenues are freed up for economic development objectives. In particular, the Equalization Grant system is intended to direct revenue to provinces with a weak tax base. The sums involved in these Fiscal Arrangements are significant particularly for the Atlantic provinces, for whom they amount to around one-half of total revenues. The Arrangements are subject to a quinquennial review.[13]

In a static sense, the Fiscal Arrangements Act, which redistributes national revenues to the poorer provinces is clearly beneficial to these provinces, and helps to encourage local investment. But in a dynamic sense, it is impossible to compare this situation with one in which provinces were independent in terms of revenue raising but also in terms of development strategy. Some of the policy issues involved are explored in chapter five.

3.9 CONCLUSION

It has been demonstrated in this chapter how the pattern of Canadian financial development was strongly influenced by the sequence of development of the Canadian economy as well as by external factors. While the Maritimes was the first area to be settled, the need for credit spawned a simultaneous financial development in Upper Canada, Lower Canada and the Maritimes. When Maritime industry (fishing, boatbuilding, etc.) suffered a decline at the end of the nineteenth century, Central Canada's financial pre-eminence was assured. With the shift westward of the economic axis, particularly in the 1970s, Western Canada for a period acquired its own banks, but Central Canada remains the home of Canada's financial centre. The period of consolidation of the financial system had happened to coincide with Toronto and Montreal's period of economic eminence. Their continued influence over the financial system has been reinforced by the centralising tendency of Canada's non-bank financial intermediaries.

The rôle and behaviour of national financial institutions has been a matter of contention in each of the regions surveyed. In each case, the ability of a nationwide branch banking system to facilitate capital outflows has been identified as a potentially impoverishing factor. Against this had to be weighed the benefits of a stable banking system, whose strength was not dependent on the economic conditions of any one region, with the facility to generate capital inflows. There the similarity ends. The typical response in each of the three regions has been conditioned by that region's historical experience. It is notable that at both the theory and policy levels, discussion of the implications of a concentrated national financial system has been conducted quite separately for each region, with little cross-reference.

In the Maritimes, there are in fact two distinct interpretations. That adopted by policy-makers is that the Maritimes' economic problems stem from relatively unattractive investment opportunities. Risk-averse bank lending behaviour combined with national monetary policy geared to economic conditions elsewhere further discourage investment. The solution lies in marginal changes in the behaviour of public and private financial institutions to encourage investment, improving the risk-profile of Maritime business. By implication, following a transitional period, the Maritimes would no longer require special treatment.

In contrast, the dependency theorists see the concentration of industry and finance in Central Canada as an inherent feature of capitalist economies. Marginal changes would not alter that historical tendency; rather structural changes in the organisation of the financial sector would be required, particularly the development of locally-owned financial institutions.

Quebec until recently contained a major financial centre. Only with the recent relative decline of Montreal's share of Canada's financial market has a serious examination of the regional effects of the financial system taken place. As a result, the Quebec analysis does not reflect the dependency theory notion of an inevitable tendency towards concentration. The policy proposals emerging from the Quebec studies reflect an optimism that government intervention can reverse the decline of Montreal; thereafter market forces can be allowed to allocate financial resources efficiently. In particular, the analysis has concentrated on the distribution of financial services within Canada, not extending the argument to encompass the international distribution, so that increased freedom of international capital flows is urged by several studies. The underlying theory is not, therefore, a general theory of financial interrelationships, but is specific to those between Ontario and Quebec.

The Western region's settlement and economic development did not take place until after the consolidation of the financial system in Central Canada. Unlike the Maritimes and Quebec, therefore, there was no experience of local financial control before concentration of the financial system in Toronto. Thus, while Western analysis focused on the national redistribution of funds through the financial system, policy proposals could not be geared to reversing the demise of local financial institutions. The structural approach adopted by dependency theorists in the Maritimes, therefore, was adopted in some form in the West right across the political spectrum. Experience of the national financial system in Western Canada, particularly during the Depression years, suggested that marginal adaptations of market forces would have at most marginal effects. Rather provincial government intervention, in the form of equity in chartered banks or direct control over provincial money supply, was required to alter the regional allocation of financial resources.

Much of this analysis has been strongly influenced by experience with the regional distribution of the national credit total in the early stages of banking development. This experience was particularly acute in a country like Canada whose rapid economic development was associated with regional settlement and where credit needs, given the investment opportunities available, were great. It is no doubt for this reason that the issue of the regional impact of banking structure has been so important historically in both Canada and the United States, compared with longer-established economies.

But the issue has been diffused in recent years with the consciousness that regional credit creation is no longer limited by national reserves constraints, far less regional reserves constraints. The issue is no longer one of the regional distribution of a national total. And yet the behaviour of centralised financial institutions with respect to credit creation in different regions is still of considerable importance; the recent brief experience with a proliferation of small, regionally based banks has not altered the dominance of the Big Five banks.

In the next chapter we consider in much more detail the regional pattern of credit creation and the financial preferences and behaviour of all sectors in the context of the current, fifth, stage of banking development. With the complexities of sophisticated financial markets in this latest stage of banking development, the regional patterns are much less stable than in Canada's earlier years. Yet, now that the financial investment opportunities for all sectors are so diverse, and so centralised, the increased scope for capital outflows from regions perceived to be in decline can compound the reluctance of banks to create credit in such regions.

Footnotes

[1]   Shortt (1896) maintains that the American was the stronger influence, the First Bank of the United States being a model for Canada's first banks. But the fact that that bank was in turn modelled on the Bank of England, that many of the key personnel in the Canadian banks were formerly British and that the British authorities actively oversaw the Canadian banking system (see Breckenridge 1894, pp.53-7) demonstrates the strength of the British influence.

[2]   The first bank was formed (unchartered) in Montreal in 1792, but failed. The Montreal Bank was formed in 1817 and received its charter as the Bank of Montreal in 1822. The Bank of New Brunswick was the first to receive its charter in 1820. The Halifax Banking Company was formed in 1825 and had a monopoly of banking until 1832, but was not chartered until 1875.

[3]   Frost's (1982) analysis of Bank of Nova Scotia records confirms the perception that a net outflow of funds from the Maritimes occurred through the Bank's inter-regional operations. He counters Acheson's (1972) argument that the Bank failed to meet the needs of local industry, which had to fall back on self-financing, on the grounds that the 1888 recession had raised the expected risk of default on bank loans to prohibitive levels.

[4]   See Overton (1978) on Newfoundland and Barrett (1980) who reviews the range of approaches taken to analysing underdevelopment in the Atlantic region in general.

[5]   See Sacouman (1981). He sees the centralization of finance capital as a central feature of Marxist analysis of the Maritimes economy. While there has been a political response, particularly on the part of labour, he explains the lack of academic analysis of this response by the fact that its expression was through civil rather than state mechanisms.

[6]   See also Benton (1974). While some bank loans are covered by government guarantee, the chartered banks still account for around 80% of all loans to small business in Canada. See Canadian Bankers' Association (1980).

[7]   The following is the view expressed by a banker in 1927 of his fellow-bankers quoted by Neufeld (1964, p.170): 'Their professional training has interfered with the success of many bank officers who have tried other lines of business after years "inside the counter". They are always looking for the possible loss instead of the possible gain'.

[8]   The union of Upper and Lower Canada of 1841 was called the Province of Canada until Confederation in 1867.

[9]   See, for example C.D. Howe Research Institute (1977) and, in a broader framework, Maxwell and Pestieau (1980), on the flows of funds through the provincial government accounts, Government of Canada (1979) for a federal study of the breakdown of capital flows, and Raynauld (1980). The data sources will be explored in some detail in Chapter 4.

[10]   Ryba (1974a) is summarised in Ryba (1974b), and in Ryba (1976).

[11]   See Benson (1978) for a study of government involvement in banking in British Columbia.

[12]   See Eaton and Bond (1970) for a discussion of the subsequent development of a new money market in Vancouver.

[13]   For a thorough discussion of the issues prior to the last review, see Economic Council of Canada (1982a).

4 The aggregative evidence from the later stages of financial development

4.1 INTRODUCTION

It has been shown in chapter three how the Canadian financial system became centralised, very early in its history, in Toronto and Montreal, with a high concentration in a few large, national institutions. Neither the temporary shift westward of the economic axis in the 1970s, nor the growing importance of non-bank financial intermediaries has fundamentally altered that pattern. It has been shown also that the various sectors in the regions other than Ontario and Quebec and latterly also Quebec, have perceived themselves to be at a disadvantage in obtaining finance. The various studies conducted at the micro level (such as Brym and Sacouman 1979, and Acheson 1977) support this perception.

The focus of this chapter is on the more recent, aggregative evidence. The conventional statement about this evidence refers to comparisons of bank assets and liabilities by province:

> Regional needs are served equitably(Canadian Bankers' Association 1978)

The existence in Canada of provincial differences between bank loans and deposits is evidence that banks are doing their job in a non-discriminatory manner (Benson 1978).

It is the main purpose of this chapter to challenge both the accuracy and relevance of these statements.

Up to World War II, when there was no Canadian lender-of-last-resort, regional credit growth was determined as a share of a national total. This is no longer the case. Nevertheless, credit growth in one region is still not independent of economic conditions in other regions, nor of the structure of the financial system. Centralisation of credit decisions is influenced by perceptions at the Centre of credit-worthiness in the Periphery, which in turn is influenced by industrial structure (whether or not the borrower is headquartered in Centre, for example). Credit-worthiness, and indeed the demand for credit, are in turn influenced by liquidity preference; high liquidity preference in the Periphery reduces the willingness of Periphery residents to buy local assets rather than Centre assets, thus actually reducing the availability of liquidity.

The outcome of these factors is low credit growth in Periphery relative to Centre, except during boom periods when expected Periphery returns are likely to be exaggerated. Relatively high liquidity preference in Periphery, which prevails except in boom conditions, is manifested by relatively high capital outflows. As a result, income growth will be relatively weak. Also the preference for Centre assets may be thwarted by the need to realise liquidity for working capital, which makes it difficult to identify unconstrained preferences.

Indeed, it is not at all straightforward to interpret aggregative data in order to assess whether or not this is a valid representation of reality. What we have set out above (and in more detail in chapter two) is a process: a process, moreover, which is fuelled by perceptions and expectations governed by the unquantified conventions of the relevant group (Periphery firms, Centre banks, etc.).[1] In effect, it is being argued here that the demand for liquidity and its supply are interdependent, where a major factor in their interdependence is an unquantified, expectations, variable. The result is an identification problem, whereby it is difficult to identify separable demand and supply functions; this would otherwise have been the standard approach to interpreting the evidence.[2] Resolution of the identification problem is rendered virtually impossible by the difficulty involved in quantifying the expectations variables which would shift both functions simultaneously. More generally, it is extremely difficult, if not impossible to settle the question of what constitute the causal forces behind a process on the basis purely of statistical techniques.[3] The approach adopted therefore will be to examine data series for tendencies in order to shed light on our discussion of causal processes. This is an approach justified in general by Lawson (1989), but with particular justification in the context of a process as complex and dynamic as that under discussion here.

Specifically in terms of the issues addressed here, there is an insurmountable identification problem when the demand for and supply of liquidity are interdependent, and when the primary common causal variable is changes in unquantifiable expectations. If a wave of pessimism about returns on assets causes the demand for liquidity to increase and its supply decrease, it is quite possible for no change in liquidity holdings to be observed.

Evidence of differing regional interest rates could be interpreted as supporting our approach but, as will be discussed below, interest rates too are subject to an identification problem. Interest differentials reflect perceived relative default risk as well as demand and supply conditions. In regional monetary theory, it is conventional to *equate* differentials with risk premia. The risk and demand and supply conditions components cannot be identified. As a corollary, it is difficult to identify the degree to which credit may be rationed, i.e. the degree to which there is unsatisfied excess demand for credit. Once the possibility of rationing is introduced,[4] then the actual allocation of credit can no longer be identified as reflecting the pattern of demand for credit. A net flow of funds out of a region is consistent with an excess demand for credit. This contrasts with the conventional identification of outflows of funds with excess supply.

Because of these difficulties in gleaning direct evidence of financial constraints in expenditure in different regions, the alternative avenue is evidence of the financial behaviour which, it has been suggested, underlies those financial constraints. To the extent that this behaviour itself is unconstrained, it would allow some conclusion as to the validity of the theory presented here relative to conventional regional monetary theory.

In pursuing this course we encounter the second major difficulty, the limited quality of regional data. On the surface, Canada appears to be relatively fortunate in the quality and range of its regional financial data. On closer inspection, however, the data have serious limitations, many of which are unavoidable in an integrated national economy. First, while the Bank of Canada publishes quarterly data on the provincial breakdown of bank balance sheets (on a complete basis, from 1976), a good estimate of the regional deposits and loans cannot be made. The allocation of deposit holdings to each province is based on the location of the deposit, not the location of the depositor. In particular, Ontario deposits will include unspecified amounts of deposits of residents of other provinces who have accounts in the financial centre, Toronto. Similarly, the allocation of bank loans is determined by the location of the lending bank branch, not of the borrower, or of the location in which the loan is extended.

Further, changes in regional liquidity due to net payments imbalance with other regions cannot be derived from the provincial accounts data published by Statistics Canada (for the period from 1961). Other things being equal, net exports of goods and services are by definition offset exactly by net capital flows [5] (positive net exports indicating a net capital outflow). But the net exports item in the case of the Canadian provincial accounts combines net exports to the overseas sector with those to the rest of Canada, and it includes the residual error of each province's accounts (an error which can be of considerable magnitude in a statistical minefield like provincial accounting).

The usefulness of the provincial banking and accounting data is thus severely limited. They have however been used in the recent debates over regional financial flows both at the political level [6] and the academic level.[7] We therefore consider in the next section what if any conclusions may legitimately be drawn from them. The limited information on regional interest rates is also considered in this section.

The third section is devoted to assessing the argument that there are disparities in financial efficiency among the regions. This argument was used in chapter two to suggest that liquidity preference would be satisfied better by financial centre assets than financial assets issued elsewhere; regardless of regional differences in liquidity preference, this would lead to financial flows drawn to the financial centre. (The allocation of financial assets by the financial centre is another matter.) The asset distribution of households and corporations is considered in the following two sections for indications of different regional liquidity preference. Then the behaviour of financial institutions themselves is considered in section six. This behaviour is analysed, in terms of *creating* the financial instruments which lead to inter-regional financial flows rather than redistributing existing instruments.

What we wish to investigate then, within the limitations of the data, is the regional pattern of credit creation and liquidity preference. While the argument so far has been expressed along the lines of relatively 'low' and 'high' credit creation, implicit has been the notion of 'low' or 'high' relative to what would be warranted by informed expectations as to returns on investment, which, unfortunately, are unquantified. So, while we will set out what information is available, it is unlikely to be informative. More promising is the scope for finding evidence of differing liquidity preference, albeit constrained.

The data series for different variables are available, as will become apparent, for widely different periods, some quarterly and some annually. Since some of the series are available only for around the last ten years, the scope for useful econometric work, distinguishing the experience of the different regions (far less provinces) under different economic conditions is extremely limited at this stage. What we can do here is to survey what is available, discussing some of the complexities of interpreting the data, thus laying the groundwork for future econometric work once a full set of data is available for sufficiently long periods.

The data discussed here, and set out in the Appendix, are therefore designed primarily to be indicative of what is available. At the same time, however, the particular years shown (where possible) have been selected to show representative regional cross-sections, over a fifteen year span, under very different national economic conditions. Thus 1966 and 1976 were chosen as years of national prosperity, and 1970 and 1980 as years of national recession. This allows some degree of normalisation. Further, it will be informative not only to compare regions within each of the selected years, but also to compare the regional pattern in 1966 and 1976 with 1970 and 1980, and to get some idea of secular trends. (The number of available observations is, of course, much too limited for these comparisons to be made on anything other than a basis of casual empiricism; this reinforces the need for a pluralist, political economy methodology.) Each region's experience differs somewhat over the cycle; here the major exceptions are the Atlantic region's good income performance in 1970 and the Prairie region's good performance in 1980. (The income data for each region, and for Canada as a whole, are shown in Table 4.1.) By comparing portfolios for each region at cycle peaks and troughs it is hoped that some perception of constrained and relatively unconstrained behaviour will be possible.

Finally, the regional breakdown reflects a grouping of administrative units (provinces) into economic regions: the four Atlantic provinces and the three Prairie provinces are amalgamated into two groups. This conventional classification is chosen because it reflects both data availability (although most of the data are also available by province) and political institutional realities. Each region nevertheless covers wide disparities. In the Prairie region, for example, strong income growth related to oil and gas activity in the 1970s is concentrated in Alberta and Saskatchewan, with Manitoba lagging behind. More significantly for a Metropolis-Hinterland analysis, it is only the Golden Horseshoe of Ontario which constitutes the Metropolis, the rest having more in common with Manitoba and Northern Quebec. Nevertheless, analysis conducted at the regional level is legitimate to the extent that sectors perceive their own regional identity; there are, for example, systematic differences between the expectations which borrowers and lenders form with respect to different regions.

Canadian regional disparities, measured by per capita Gross Provincial Product (GPP) have maintained a consistent pattern over a long period. (See Table 4.2.) Since the 1960s, for example, the Atlantic region's GPP per capita has hovered around sixty per cent of the national average, Quebec around ninety per cent, and Ontario and BC around 110%. The Prairie region has seen the widest fluctuations. The boom in the 1970s primarily reflected increases in the volume and value of oil and gas production, and was thus interpreted (correctly, in retrospect) by Norrie and Percy (1981) and by Phillips (1982) as a cyclical staple boom rather than the beginning of a secular trend.

We turn now to consider the macro evidence in more detail.

4.2 THE MACRO EVIDENCE

The macro evidence most frequently considered in relation to finance and regional development is the net position of the banking sector in each province. Neufeld defended the banks against neo-Marxist criticisms of draining capital from regions in his evidence in 1980 to the Standing Senate Committee on National Finance: 'Almost all regions have been a net receiver of funds. The big exception is Ontario. Ontario has been supplying funds to all the other regions.' (Government of Canada, 1982, issue No. 6, p.6:10). In the case of his evidence to the same Committee (Government of Canada, 1982, p.92) the regional share of the national total of bank loans relative to the regional share of GDP was the comparison made. An excess of bank assets over liabilities in lower-income regions and a higher share of loans than of GDP in lower-income regions has been used as evidence of the convergence-promoting activities of the national banking system.

The comparison of regional shares of total bank assets with liabilities does indeed show a general pattern of assets in excess of liabilities for lower-income provinces. (See Table 4.3.) However, although the banks have allocated all their assets and liabilities provincially, some can only be done artificially, by formula (such as holdings of securities). It is more informative, therefore, to consider only those assets and liabilities which have a fairly clear regional identification. (The items thus selected are discussed in Section 4.6 and shown in Tables 4.25 to 4.28.) These data too show the share of assets in excess of liabilities for the Atlantic region, and marginally so for Quebec, in late 1976 and 1980 their share of assets being lower in the less favourable climate of 1980. However, although 1980 was nationally a low growth year, the Prairies were enjoying a natural resource boom, reflected in an increased share of assets relative to liabilities. BC's slight increase in share of assets stayed steady, in excess of liabilities in both years. Ontario had a higher share of liabilities than assets in both years. Both Ontario and BC increased their share of liabilities i.e. successfully increased liquidity in the poorer conditions of 1980. (See Table 4.4.) The trends in bank lending mirror the trends in regional shares of GDP (in Table 4.5). Moreover, the Atlantic and Prairie regions and BC's share of bank loans exceeded their share of GDP while that of Ontario and Quebec fell short.

Considering these data in terms of shares of national totals is useful, in that it abstracts from fluctuations in the national totals. But it does suggest an interpretation more appropriate to earlier stages in the banking system, in terms of distributions of national totals by means of inter-regional transfers. In the context of the modern banking system, the interpretation should start rather with credit creation, and its effect on regional liquidity and economic activity. By this interpretation, the data suggest that both the liquidity and income generated by credit in the Atlantic and Prairie regions and BC are markedly less than Ontario and Quebec. The only benchmark, then, by which to measure credit creation is the regional distribution of population (shown in Table 4.6), which shows credit creation high in both years in per capita terms in the Prairies and BC and low in Quebec and the Atlantic region.

In order to pursue further the different consequences of credit creation in each region (which in turn must influence subsequent credit creation), we must consider now the pattern of inter-regional financial flows, trade flows and returns on investment.

In accounting terms, the flow of private sector funds between regions is measured as the difference between savings and investment in each region *ex post* (i.e. actual values, not necessarily preferred values). In aggregate, expenditure in a region's economy must equal uses of income:

$$C + I + G + X - M = C + S + T \quad \dots\dots\dots\dots\dots\dots \quad (4.1)$$

where expenditure is made up consumption (C), investment (I), government spending (G) and exports less imports (X-M), and income is used for consumption, saving (S) and taxation (T). Rearranging terms and eliminating consumption from both sides:

$$(S-I) = (G-T) + (X-M) \quad \dots\dots\dots\dots\dots\dots\dots \quad (4.2)$$

Any difference between saving and investment in a region must equal the sum of the government budgetary deficit or surplus and the trade deficit or surplus; when savings are high relative to investment, the excess finances either or both of a budgetary deficit and a trade surplus.

In Statistics Canada's experimental provincial accounts, the government sector's accounts are on a payments rather than benefits basis, which is suitable for an analysis of flows of funds.[8] The net exports estimates however are derived as a residual, by subtracting all other expenditure accounts calculation, it is on the admission of Statistics Canada [9] the weakest element in the accounts.

It is possible nevertheless to say something about two factors influencing the size and sign of the residual item, because of the way in which the accounts are constructed. First, it was not possible to identify tourist expenditure in each region, so that consumption includes tourist expenditures by visitors from other regions which would normally be included in exports. For net tourist expenditures in a region to be transferred to the net exports component, the residual has to include the negative amount of the tourist expenditures. For regions normally in net surplus on the travel account, therefore, the surplus on current account (X-M) is understated (or the deficit overstated). The Atlantic region and BC are the two most likely candidates for a net tourist surplus.

Second, the accounts are on a domestic basis, i.e. they measure income earned in the region by both residents and non-residents, and excludes income earned elsewhere by residents. Income on a 'national' basis, measuring all income earned by residents, would thus be greater in the case of net inflows of interest and dividends, which in turn reflect capital outflows in the past. If the expenditure accounts were to be changed to a 'national' basis, so that 'net exports' would include net receipts of interest and dividends, then net exports would be higher for regions which had been net lenders of funds in the past. The residual thus includes the negative of net receipts of interest and dividends; net exports is understated for net lenders; which regions are net lenders is one of the facts we wish to establish.

Even with this information about two components of the residual, there will still be a residual element arising from the difficulty of constructing regional data. The data for the government budgetary balance (T-G) and net exports plus residual item (X-M+*e*) are shown in Tables 4.7 and 4.8. Using equation (4.2), we can now produce an estimate for savings minus investmesnt plus residual item (S-I+*e*) in Table 4.9. All are shown as a percentage of Gross Provincial Product as a normalising procedure.

The public sector (all levels of government) was in substantial deficit in the Atlantic region in all four of the selected years. The deficit position of the Prairies turned into a surplus in 1976 and 1980; an important element was increasing oil revenues. At the same time, the federal oil subsidy put the oil consuming regions east of the Prairies into deficit over the same period. The trade balance plus residual was in substantial deficit in the Atlantic region, and in gradually declining surplus in Ontario, over the period, with Quebec moving into deficit in 1976 and the Prairies into surplus in 1970 and BC in 1980. This is consistent with the relatively low income growth generated by bank credit in the Atlantic region compared with the more favourable position in Ontario i.e. a high import content to Atlantic expenditure reduced the value of the income multiplier.

The balance of payments position reflected in net exports refers to the payments both between regions and other countries; the capital flows implicit in Table 4.9 thus include international as well as interregional flows. While net private sector capital flows for Canada as a whole are known from the national accounts, there is no satisfactory way of allocating them region-by-region without begging several questions. We can thus only draw (very tentative) conclusions about whether regions are net lenders or borrowers, not about the source of direction of flows of funds.

Given the data limitations, the only admissible conclusion in fact is that net capital flows are not large relative to income for any region. The public sector deficit finances so much of the trade imbalance (plus residual) that the difference between the two, set out in Table 4.9, indicates a much lesser rôle for private sector capital flows, relative to income. The two regions shown with most negative proportions of income are the Atlantic region and BC, the two most likely to have capital outflows overstated on account of the tourism balance. For a high income region like Ontario, with large tourist expenditures elsewhere, the reverse is likely to be true. For those regions which have been net lenders in the past, capital outflows are understated by the sum of net interest and dividend receipts. If current net lending is an indication of past net lending, this factor suggests that net flows are understated by Table 4.9.

These estimates of net capital flows (the negative of the amounts in Table 4.9) can be compared with the net intra-bank flows represented by the difference between bank assets and liabilities within each region. These are shown as a percentage of GPP in Table 4.10. For all the drawbacks with the provincial accounts data and the banking data, it is noticeable how much larger the intra-bank flows are than the estimates of total net capital flows between regions. What this implies is that there were *large capital outflows from the Atlantic region and Quebec and from the Prairies in 1980 other than through the banks, reflecting high liquidity preference and/or low expected returns in these regions.*

An additional indicator of net regional savings can be derived directly from the personal savings and investment data of the provincial accounts. Because the personal savings data are derived from expenditure data which include tourist expenditure by non-residents, savings are understated for regions with a surplus on the tourism account (most likely the Atlantic region and BC). With this caveat, subtracting investment from personal saving shows the degree of financing of private sector investment by both corporate retained earnings and capital inflows. If retained earnings as a proportion of GPP were of a similar magnitude in all regions, then these data (set out in Table 4.11) imply a net inflow of capital to the Atlantic region, BC, and the Prairie region (after 1970 at any rate) from Quebec and Ontario.

It would not be at all surprising for total savings to be close to investment. Observed savings are the *outcome* of income generated by actual investment, neither savings nor investment necessarily equalling their planned magnitudes. If the income multiplier and thus the propensity to save are stable, then a given amount of investment in a region will generate savings according to a stable relationship. How much investment takes place is determined in part by corporate savings, but also by the allocation of new credit, particularly when profits are low and corporate saving constrained. The multiplier will be higher the lower the propensities to import and to save. Import leakages redirect the credit created to finance the investment to the exporting economies, while the relative attractiveness of existing assets issued locally and in other regions determines how new savings choices redirect the new funds.

While the creation and distribution of credit influences the distribution of money holdings, the identification problem prevents us from distinguishing between holdings which result from competing shifts of demand and supply on the one hand, and uniform stable regional demand on the other, i.e. between a Post Keynesian theory and a neo-classical theory. Indeed, the regional banking data are consistent with either theory. (See Table 4.12.) Bank chequing deposits were around ten per cent of regional income in 1976 and eight per cent in 1980 (reflecting higher national interest rates). Total bank deposits show more regional variance in both years. But even then no conclusions can be reached as to the significance of this variance since Ontario deposits particularly are overstated by non-resident deposits. The increase in the ratio of total deposits to GPP in all regions in 1980 from the 1976 level does confirm an increase in liquidity preference at the same time as economic conditions deteriorate. However, it is also consistent with Friedman's argument that stable demand for money with respect to permanent income entails pro-cyclical velocity of circulation with respect to actual income.

Turning to interest rates for some information on whether observed financial conditions reflect stable demand and accommodating supply, or not, we are limited to two sources: mortgage interest rates and provincial government bond yields. Even if banks published the actual interest rates charged on loans, systematic regional differences could not be interpreted as reflecting differences in regional market conditions. Banks have a structure of interest rates which is applied to all regions, with higher rates charged for such factors as higher default risk, higher administrative costs per dollar of loan, etc. Since estimation of these factors is partly subjective, it allows leaway for a manager to choose a lower rate in a region where demand for loans fell short of supply and a higher rate where demand exceeded supply. Since our theory implies that excess demand occurs in the Periphery, particularly when economic conditions are expected to deteriorate, it will also coincide with increased perceived default risk. The two are impossible to disentangle. Further, other factors entering the determination of loan rates will lead to higher charges in the Periphery: information costs are higher the more remote the region and both information and administration costs are higher per dollar of loan the smaller the loan (usually the smaller the business).[11]

The (Bryce) Royal Commission on Corporate Concentration (1978, pp.65-6) noted the higher interest charges on small business and investigated the relative performance of large and small businesses. In fact they found that large diversified corporations on average yielded lower and more variable returns to stockholders than other corporations; variability of returns is conventionally taken as a measure of risk. In contrast, the Economic Council of Canada (1982a, pp.24-5) argue that variability of return is higher the smaller the firm, although this may reflect their higher debt/equity ratio as much as variability of income. (Equity financing allows financing costs to fluctuate with income.)

Ultimate risk may be measured by propensity for bankruptcy, requiring loan default. Statistics Canada data on commercial failures, available only until 1978, show the incidence of failures by region (see Table 4.13). Relative to the number of businesses in each region (see Table 4.14, taken from data compiled for the study, Economic Council of Canada, 1982a) there is in fact a relatively high incidence of failures in Ontario and Quebec. It cannot be concluded that this evidence suggests lower default risk in all loan applications among Periphery corporate borrowers; it could be argued that the low incidence of actual failures was due to successful screening out of high risk loan applicants and/or a more generous lending policy in the Periphery towards potentially bankrupt firms. On the available evidence neither case is proven; it certainly cannot be asserted that actual default risk is higher in the Periphery, requiring a risk premium on borrowing charges. It cannot be argued therefore that higher interest charges do not in fact reflect excess demand for credit.

Interest charges on mortgage loans are a useful source of information in that the location of loan issues is most likely to be the location of the borrower and of the expenditure of the loan. Further, since the National Housing Association (NHA) in approving loans reduces default risk, interest rate differentials are more likely to reflect market conditions. The Canadian Mortgage and Housing Corporation (CMHC) published for some years a regional breakdown of mortgage rates. For 1966, rates were shown by type of lender, along with information on the average term of loan by type of lender; there is no systematic relationship between term and mortgage rates. (See Table 4.15.) For institutions specialising in mortgage lending, rates charged in the Atlantic region were above average, all other regions being below average. Ontario has slightly above average rates only from other, non-corporate lenders, a category which is dominated by credit unions which are not so important as a source of funds in Ontario. The Atlantic region borrowers pay above average rates to all lenders. The same relative pattern holds for 1970 and 1976. The widening disparities in 1976 must be accounted for, at least in part, by higher interest rates at the national level and growing scope for differing inflationary expectations.

Perhaps more revealing are the terms on which provincial governments borrow on the United States market. Governments are rated by the underwriting agents according to default risk; there is a well-known systematic relationship between rating and interest rates charged [11] although market conditions, term to maturity etc. also influence interest rates. There is a close correspondence between rating and relative income (see Tables 4.2 and 4.16) although the Canadian government's rating always matches that of the highest-rated province. The ratings gradually improved over the period covered, although the recession was prompting actual or potential downward revisions by 1983. Yields vary depending on the length to maturity and the time of year relative to interest payments and hence, where several issues were outstanding, the mid-point of the range is shown. Generally, with these provisos, yields are higher when ratings are higher.[12]

The notion of differing default risk is interesting to contemplate when considering the influence, on the terms of credit, of borrower's perceptions. There is no recent history of provincial government defaults on which to base a probability of default in the future. Nor is it conceivable that the federal government would now allow a provincial default situation to arise. Indeed the Revenue Stabilization Program requires the federal government to provide financial assistance to any province experiencing an absolute fall in income, with some qualification with respect to natural resource revenues. (See Government of Canada, 1977.) The intergovernmental environment is somewhat different in the United States and perhaps leads lenders there to apply the same risk expectations to Canadian provinces as to State governments. If this misperception of the nature of Canadian inter-governmental relations does not explain ratings differentials (and thus rate differentials) then the only remaining explanation is tighter financial conditions in poorer regions, as suggested in chapter two.[13]

The perceptions in the financial centre of economic conditions in the Periphery are significant for the regional allocation of credit by financial institutions. Regional flows of funds are also influenced by the relative attractiveness of existing financial assets in different regions. Here the relative sophistication of financial institutions in each region plays a rôle. In the next section we examine the evidence on the regional distribution of Canada's financial sector, having concluded from the evidence outlined in this section, that credit demand is constrained in lower-income regions.

4.3 THE REGIONAL COMPOSITION OF THE FINANCIAL SECTOR

In chapter three the financial sector was described as becoming concentrated in Toronto and Montreal, particularly since the turn of the century, with Montreal losing ground from the second world war. In this section we consider what significance this has had for the provision of financial services in the regions. Three indicators are available: the regional distribution of employment in the financial sector (Table 4.17) and of branches of banks and other deposit-taking institutions (Table 4.18) and the rate of turnover of deposits (Table 4.19).

Employment in finance, insurance and real estate in Ontario in each year exceeds both income and population shares (see Tables 4.5 and 4.6), confirming the perception that Ontario houses a major share of financial business in Canada. While Quebec's share marginally exceeds its income share, the margin had almost disappeared by 1980, reflecting the relative decline in importance of Montreal. By 1976 the financial employment share was already lower than the population share. The Atlantic region is consistently low in financial employment relative to population particularly. Even the Prairies' employment share, which increased over the period, lags behind both income and population growth. BC's financial sector employs less than is warranted by income share, but more than is warranted by population share.

Concentration is much less evident from the distribution of branches of financial institutions, particularly when other deposit-taking institutions than banks are included in the total. Branches distribution corresponds fairly closely to population distribution; the greater incidence in the Prairies is to be expected given the higher incidence of small, scattered communities. The disparity between the financial sector employment and the branch data (other than accounted for by institutions covered by the employment data but not by the branch data) indicate the difference in type of branch predominant in each region. In Ontario particularly, each branch serves a relatively large population, concentrated in urban areas, employing larger, more specialised staffs. Indeed Kerr (1965) argues that employment and branch data are misleading as indicators of financial activity; it is the concentration of functions other than retail banking in Toronto and Montreal which reflect the degree of effective concentration in these two centres.

Specialisation and concentration in the financial sector increase opportunities for earning returns on idle money balances, i.e. increase the opportunity cost of holding idle balances. An indication of the degree to which balances are kept active is provided by the rate of turnover of chequing deposits, using cheque cashing data (see Table 4.19). Whichever aggregate of chequing deposits is used, banks, with credit unions and caisses populaires, with savings institutions or with mortgage companies and trust companies, the picture is clear: turnover in Ontario is consistently higher than in other regions. Quebec comes second according to most measures. In all cases the rate of turnover is lowest in the Atlantic region.

Care must be taken with interpreting these data. It is not a significant problem that deposits are allocated by location of financial institution rather than residence of holder; indeed the opportunities for financial investment for which turnover may be used as a proxy would imply that a sizeable proportion of Quebec and Ontario deposits are held by non-residents. But the clearing data themselves are problematic in that they do not reflect clearings *within* institutions, only those *between* institutions. Only if we assume that the extensive national branch network of the largest banks prevents any serious regional bias in the data can the overall pattern be taken to reflect total turnover rates. United States clearings data are more accurate because, with a unit banking system, a higher proportion of clearings are interbank and thus recorded. These data in fact confirm the impression that deposits are used more actively the closer the proximity to the financial centre.[14]

The interest rate evidence in section two implied higher loan charges the lower per capita income while the turnover data imply higher returns on financial acsets the better the access to the financial centre. We now proceed to glean some evidence on the borrowing and lending behaviour of three sectors, household, business and financial, in the light of these regional differences in financial conditions.

4.4 THE PORTFOLIO BEHAVIOUR OF THE HOUSEHOLD SECTOR

Given the relative poverty of information at the fully aggregated, macro level, it may be possible to observe regional patterns in portfolio behaviour for different sectors which would allow some conclusions to be drawn about the direction of capital flows under different circumstances. The discussion in chapter two suggests that all sectors in low-income regions attempt to keep portfolios more liquid than high-income regions but, particularly in economic downturns, are thwarted by supply constraints.

The data available on household portfolios arise from three sources: the liability structure, by region, of financial institutions, Revenue Canada data an investment income and capital gains and losses as reported for tax purposes, and the Statistics Canada surveys of household assets. It is difficult with any of these sources to establish categorically the structure of household portfolios but we consider each in turn to glean what information we can.

First, deposit institutions (to be discussed in more detail in the sixth section) publish data indicating the distribution of personal funds between demand deposits, savings deposits and time deposits. However a high ratio of demand deposits to savings deposits, for example, cannot necessarily be taken as an indication of a more liquid portfolio; the information has to be taken along with information on less liquid assets. Relatively low savings deposits could reflect a switch into bonds as much as a switch into demand deposits (see Dow and Earl 1982, chapter two). Chartered banks' personal demand deposits and personal savings deposits data indicate that the Atlantic region, the Prairies and BC accounted for a relatively higher share of demand deposits than savings deposits in both 1976 and 1980 (see Table 4.2). The theory in chapter two would suggest that this reflected demand factors in the Atlantic region, and supply factors in the other two regions. Both the Prairies and BC increased their share of both types of deposit between 1976 and 1980. The Atlantic region's holding of bank deposits is high relative to its share of national income (see Table 4.5) again consistent with relatively high liquidity preference.

The second source of information is Revenue Canada Taxation's data on unearned income declared for tax purposes, which allows a breakdown by bank interest, bond interest, dividends and net capital gains (which, unfortunately, exclude capital gains on owner-occupied houses) (see Table 4.21). It is to be expected that lower-income households prefer primarily income-earning assets to less liquid assets which nevertheless hold out the chance of capital gain. (See Robinson, 1952.) And indeed the share of income accounted for by net capital gains is positively correlated with per capita income, the largest shares being in the Prairies and BC where actual gains on a given dollar value of local assets (quite apart from the proportion of such assets held) would be high during that boom period. The reduced share of high retired population, giving the province the highest per capita net worth level in both years. (See Statistics Canada 13-547 and 13-572.) Otherwise, Ontario households had the lowest liquid asset ratio in both years.

4.5 THE PORTFOLIO BEHAVIOUR OF CORPORATIONS

There are no published data on corporate financial structure by region, although there are data on financial structure by firm size and by industry. The Economic Council of Canada has however classified the Statistics Canada corporate data by location of head office, allowing some regional analysis.

The conclusion they reach is that regional differences in financial structure are more influenced by differences in firm size and industry than by location of the corporation's head office. (See Economic Council of Canada, 1982a, p.27.) Remoteness from financial centres, particularly among small and medium sized businesses, is nonetheless given in the report as a factor influencing the cost, and to a greater extent the availability, of bank credit. So, unless the amount of credit influences the scale of balance sheets rather than their composition, we would in fact expect location in a remote area to influence financial structure. Indeed, the theory put forward here suggests that businesses in the Periphery attempt to maintain relatively liquid portfolios (more liquid assets, less liquid liabilities) while at the same time the supply of liquidity is limited. Again we face an identification problem.

Some of the data from the Economic Council of Canada (1982a) study have been made available in frequency distribution form, by region, providing some indication of corporate financial structure by region in 1976. The data allow the Metropolitan areas of Quebec and Ontario to be shown separately, with the remainder shown as an additional Hinterland region, 'Northern Quebec and Northern Ontario'. Although 1976 was a good year in terms of real income growth, that was a disparate corporate experience. Corporate profits before taxes were 16% of GPP in the Prairies, 10% in Ontario and BC, 9% in Quebec and 7% in the Atlantic region. (See Statistics Canada 13-213.) Financial structures cannot thus be treated as reflecting totally unconstrained preferences, for the Atlantic region at least. Taking the ratio of current assets to current liabilities as an indicator of relative liquidity, the least liquid regions are the Atlantic region, Northern Quebec and Northern Ontario and BC. (See Table 4.23.) (Although a wealthy province in terms of assets, profitability of corporations based in BC is not high.) Ontario's corporations are the most liquid by this measure. In every case, liquidity is higher for large corporations than small corporations.

A major contributory factor to small business illiquidity is the structure of financing. The Economic Council of Canada (1982a, p.21) study shows equity at 42% of assets for firms with assets of $0.25 million or less, rising steadily to 57% for firms with assets of $25 million and over. Within liabilities, the short-term component is around 70% for all sizes of firm, except for those over $25 million (52%). Among long term liabilities small firms rely more on mortgages and larger firms on debentures. But because of the lesser access to equity capital among small firms,[15] short term liabilities are high relative to total assets, as are long term liabilities, both being more liquid than equity capital for the lender and more illiquid for the corporate borrower.

The ratio of short term bank loans to total assets is highest for the Atlantic region, Northern Quebec and Northern Ontario, and also for the rest of Quebec. (See Table 4.24.) Short term bank loans are usually made on the basis of a line of credit which can be drawn on as the need arises. The loans are more liquid for the borrower the greater the risk of the line of credit being reduced or withdrawn. Given the higher interest charges on loans to small businesses in remote areas, as noted by the Royal Commission on Corporate Concentration (1978, pp.65-6) and the Economic Council of Canada (1982a, chapter three), the greater reliance on bank loans in these regions is a sign of greater illiquidity. In the Atlantic region, Quebec and BC, even large corporations are relatively reliant on short term bank loans, but if their credit lines are more secure than for small firms, those loans are a lesser indicator of illiquidity.

Certainly firm size can explain a lot of the illiquidity of Periphery regions' corporate financial structure,[16] and Periphery regions have a relatively high incidence of small business. Large corporations are concentrated in Ontario, with all other regions having a higher proportion of the national total of small corporations than large corporations. (See Table 4.24.) The cut-off point of five million dollars in assets employed by the Economic Council is in fact still fairly large; if a finer classification were available it is likely that the regional distribution would have been even more skewed.

Industrial structure must also contribute to the regional pattern of financial structure. Statistics Canada data for Canada as a whole for 1976 show the ratio of current assets to current liabilities to be 106.4% for the agriculture, forestry and fishing sector, compared to 164.4% for manufacturing; the former industry is more prevalent in the Periphery and the latter in the Centre. Construction and utilities, a more evenly distributed sector, has a ratio of 118.9%. (see Statistics Canada, 61-207.)

Statistically it may be the case, as the Economic Council suggests, that corporate financial structure is 'explained' better by factors such as firm size and industrial structure than by location of head office. It is well understood that regional categorisation is in some senses artificial. Nevertheless, regions are distinguished from each other by their economic structure. In Canada, there is a strong distinction between the Centre region around the Golden Horseshoe, with its large firms, and concentration in the manufacturing and service sectors, and the Periphery regions with more small firms and concentration in the primary sector. Because markets in primary products are more volatile than the markets for manufactured goods or for services, their assets are less liquid; they take their current value from the market value of the product. To achieve the same degree of liquidity as the manufacturing and service sectors, primary sector firms require relatively more liquid liabilities, i.e. longer-term liabilities. Yet the evidence (in Table 4.23) confirms that liquidity is lower in the regions dominated by primary production; the Prairies, with strong markets in 1976 for oil and gas products, and thus with more liquid assets, had a more liquid current assets to liabilities ratio than the other natural resource regions.

Location of firms' head offices therefore does seem to be correlated with differences in financial structure, albeit largely corresponding to the size and sectoral composition of each region. As the Economic Council report admits, before concluding that location of head office is not significant in determining financial structure, it is impossible to identify the separate supply and demand factors underlying this structure or, in their words, whether there is a credit gap. It is therefore also impossible to identify the regional composition of any such gap. It is inadmissible then to conclude that 'a firm's financial structure apparently does not depend on the location of its head office'. (Economic Council of Canada, 1982a, p.27)

We turn now to consider the portfolio behaviour of financial institutions, given the behaviour of households and corporations.

4.6 THE PORTFOLIO BEHAVIOUR OF FINANCIAL INSTITUTIONS

Financial institutions have generally been the focus of attention when the regional distribution of financial resources is under consideration. Financial institutions are constrained by the funds made available to them by household and business depositors. But the centralisation and concentration of the financial system in Canada has somewhat limited the choices open to asset holders. The power of financial institutions is generally identified as the power to collect funds and reallocate them at will.

In fact the power of financial institutions is greater if the process of deposit creation is considered more carefully. In a growing economy, with financial resources growing accordingly, the process *starts* with the expansion of credit, which then leads to a particular distribution of deposits, depending on the spending and portfolio behaviour of the recipients of the loans. Credit will be allocated where returns are highest, with allowance for risk and differential administrative costs. Of course, the notion of 'return' will not generally be a straightforward concept; it involves not only the interest charge, less default risk, but also the cultivation of profitable long-term financial relationships with clients, the maintenance of market presence to limit rival institutions' market shares, and managerial considerations.

Within a national banking system, assets and liabilities are theoretically unrelated on a regional basis; the distribution of assets is independent of the distribution of liabilities. Indeed it is impossible to assign a meaningful regional location to many assets and liabilities, particularly those administered from Head Office. They could be assigned to the Head Office region, but loans to large corporations which operate nationwide, for example, are in effect loans for expenditure in several regions. In spite of these difficulties, the banks themselves have been producing complete balance sheet data on a provincial basis from 1974, allocating national items regionally by means of formulae which are necessarily arbitrary. The difference between total assets and total liabilities by province has then been used as evidence of redistribution of funds within the banking system. In their response to the Western Economic Opportunities Conference, the Canadian Bankers' Association (1974) insisted that there was a net inflow of funds to Western Canada in 1972, since banks' total assets in the West exceeded total liabilities. Given an amount of liabilities in the West, the banks had allocated a higher amount of assets.

This conclusion cannot legitimately be drawn from the provincial balance sheet data given the fact that around half the items are allocated by formula. But even if the data were acceptable, the difference between total assets and liabilities is subject to an alternative interpretation. As we have already pointed out, if we view the banking process as generating credit which then creates deposits, we want to look at bank assets first and then see how many deposits are generated, rather than the reverse. On the face of it, the bank data show assets exceeding liabilities generally in all regions other than Ontario. This would imply that, when loans are extended outside Ontario, a significant proportion of the deposits thus created flow into Ontario either as capital flows or in payment for goods and services.

A benchmark that has been employed for assessing whether the initial allocation of credit was in some way 'fair' is the regional distribution of income. But the provision of credit is a major factor in determining that distribution since it partially determines the distribution of investment. Retained earnings are of course a major alternative source of finance. But our analysis of corporate portfolio behaviour suggests that businesses in poorer regions would prefer to retain proportionately higher earnings than in more prosperous regions, but are constrained by lower actual earnings. Thus, if anything, the availability of bank credit is a greater constraint on investment in these poorer regions.

In order to derive any evidence from the banks' provincial data, we must concentrate on those items most likely to reflect the deposits and loans of residents in a region. This means excluding all items allocated by formula, although not necessarily items such as business loans over $0.2 million, even though these are generally administered from Head Office. (See Canadian Bankers' Association, 1980.) The distribution of loans from Head Office is of great importance to credit availability in any region.

Before looking at the data in detail, it is worthwhile to discuss briefly the way in which the Canadian branch banking system is organised.[17] With respect to the assets and liabilities under its administration each branch is treated as an independent profit-maximising unit. While any shortfall is automatically made up from Head Office, the branch's profit position provides a monitoring device for managerial success or failure and for the future prospects of the branch. Just as with industrial branch plants, the profit rule is not adhered to strictly. Branches can make a 'loss' over a protracted period if their presence is necessary for maintaining or promoting share in the local market, if the local economy is known to be going through a temporary downturn, or if the region is known to be a good generator of relatively low cost deposits even if not of loan opportunities (where costs include both interest payments and administrative costs, which are lower the lower the rate of deposit turnover).

Both loans and deposits are necessary to bank profits: loans for interest revenue and deposits to allow a given level of assets to be maintained. From the banks' point of view, then, it would be not at all unreasonable to have deposit growth and loan growth as parallel or substitute success criteria for branches, with branches in some regions aiming for one rather than the other. Indeed, all bank branches are issued with deposit growth and loan growth targets. There is no *behavioural* reason why in fact banks should impose a profit criterion on most branches. The fact that the deposit and loan growth targets are combined in a profit criterion must then reflect the fact that deposits and loans are *not* independent, that it is the loan generation process which creates deposits. (We know that it is the essence of a national branch banking system that deposits do not determine allocation of credit).

How then do branch bank managers choose to allocate credit? The studies of bank lending behaviour in the Maritimes, particularly Sears' (1972) study of Nova Scotia, emphasise the importance of character as an indicator of default risk. In small communities, bank managers know their customers and are familiar with their financial capabilities. As a result, lending behaviour *can* be conservative, favouring those with established reputations at the expense of newcomers or those starting out in business. This inherent conservatism, Sears argues, is reinforced by the career structure within the banks. A manager of a branch in a community in a relatively declining area is likely to be either starting to climb the career structure or to be out of the promotion race. A loan default carries a high penalty in terms of career prospects in the first case and peace of mind in the second. While there will always be an asymmetry between the cost of a bad risk and the benefit of a good risk, that asymmetry will be greater for managers in Peripheral branches.

The growing necessity for borrowers to approach regional bank offices or Head Offices for loans, as the nominal amounts required for investment projects rise, exposes borrowers more to objective lending criteria. Further, improved training programmes for local branch managers encourage the substitution of objective criteria for character assessment at the local level. Overall, however, these trends may not be to the benefit of borrowers in Periphery. Objective criteria are based on past performance and projected performance given any planned investment projects. In the last analysis, however, no projection even of a probability can be held with absolute confidence. Keynes (1936, chapter 12) argues that, given that uncertainty, no 'objective' calculations can justify an investment project; it requires an entrepreneurial spirit to take that leap in the dark (what Keynes calls 'animal spirits'). There is no reason why bank managers should be any different in their capacity to know the future. The question then is, how regional office or Head Office loan managers form their subjective judgements to assess the 'objective criteria' compared with the local bank manager. It seems clear that the latter, with better knowledge of the local economy and of the borrower's 'character' may be able to form a better judgment, both in terms of rejecting applications from borrowers with high down-side risk and accepting those of potentially successful borrowers.

We now turn to the balance sheet data which approximate to those applicable to branches within each region. The assets for which a regional distribution can reasonably be defined constitute only 67% of the total in 1976 and 59% in 1980; the liabilities amenable to a regional distribution make up 57% and 46% of the total in 1976 and 1980, respectively. (See Tables 4.25 and 4.26.)[18] The structure of banks' local assets changed markedly between 1976 and 1980, with a switch into residential mortgage loans offsetting a switch out of personal loans. The increasing bank share of the mortgage market reflects a secular trend from 1967 when the Bank Act was amended to allow greater bank entry into the mortgage market. There was also a smaller redistribution of total (selected) assets away from provincial and municipal government finance and towards agricultural loans to farmers.

The Atlantic region received relatively low amounts of funds in residential mortgage loans, small business loans and agricultural loans to farmers, and indeed their share of small business loans fell in 1980. BC received a relatively high proportion of small business loans in both years, and the Prairie region's share increased markedly in 1980. Taking these together with loans to farmers, the Prairie region received a relatively high proportion of small loans in both years. Only one per cent of small business loans were guaranteed under the Small Business Loans Act in 1976 and four per cent in 1980; of these, Quebec and BC received a disproportionately high amount, relative to total small business loans. (See Small Business Loan Act, Annual Reports.)

Since Ontario, Quebec and the oil sector in the Prairies received a disproportionately high amount of the larger business loans compared with the Atlantic region and BC, the distribution of total bank loans was skewed in favour of the more affluent regions. Now, there is nothing untoward in this conclusion in the sense that it is to be expected that banks may judge Centre industry, and corporations engaged in a booming staple sector, as yielding highest returns with least risk. Any profit-maximising rule would steer credit in that direction rather than towards regions in financial difficulties, other things being equal. It is *possible* that the banks in fact allocate more funds to the Atlantic region, for example, than is warranted by short term profit maximising considerations. But *the evidence does support the contention that less credit is provided, relatively, to Periphery regions (barring staple product booms), especially when economic conditions worsen, and then is redirected to areas such as agriculture which are less affected by national recessions than manufacturing industry.*

Turning to the liabilities data, there was overall a reduction of liquidity in the structure of deposits between 1976 and 1980, reflected in a relative running down of demand deposits (see Tables 4.27 and 4.28.) (For the banks, such a trend increases the liquidity of a given liability total, in that proportionately less is callable on demand). This general trend was not, however, evident in the Prairie region and BC where demand deposits were built up relative to savings and time deposits. This reflects the greater ability of the regions doing relatively well in a national downturn to maintain (or build up) desired levels of liquidity. Ontario deposit totals are most likely to include deposits by non-residents, partly because of the greater degree of financial sophistication in the Metropolis. Indeed Ontario deposits are distributed more towards the high-earning instruments than in the other regions. In spite of its falling share of total income between 1976 and 1980, Ontario increased slightly its share of these selected deposits.

To the extent that the selected liabilities can be compared with the selected assets, both the Atlantic and Prairie regions retain proportionately fewer deposits relative to the loans creating new deposits in each year, while Ontario attracts relatively more deposits. If anything, this is an indication of preference for goods, services and securities purchased in Ontario, over those in the Prairie and Atlantic regions.

The view of financial institutions as creating deposits through the credit creation process applies primarily to the chartered banks, on the grounds that the 'redeposit ratio' is high; in other words, a significant proportion of financial flows arising from bank loans consist of flows back to the banks in the form of deposits. Other financial institutions traditionally are analysed simply as lending out funds deposited with them; only a small proportion of any new loans would return as deposits. Thus a new loan constitutes in effect a drawing down of reserves. The difference is, however, progressively becoming only one of degree: the relative size of the redeposit ratio.[19]

Credit unions and caisses populaires, in particular, often have a large share of a local market. To the extent that loans result in transactions between members of the same credit union or caisse populaire, the redeposit ratio will be high and credit creation will be feasible. Because membership is limited in effect to the area surrounding the location of the credit union or caisse populaire, the regional balance sheet data give a full picture of regional differences in portfolio behaviour. The portfolio composition can thus be shown, for 1976 and 1980, in terms of the distribution of regional totals of assets and liabilities within each region, rather than the regional distribution of a national total of assets and liabilities. The regional distribution of total assets is as follows: Atlantic region 2% in both years, Quebec 40% in 1976 and 46% in 1980, Ontario 17% and the Prairies 20% in both years, and BC 13% in 1976 rising to 16% in 1980. (See Tables 4.29 to 4.32.)

Credit unions and caisses populaires are provincially regulated, with some regulations specifying minimum admissible holdings of particular types of asset. Since the theory presented here is applied to all sectors, including government, we can expect these regulations to reflect each provincial government's view of appropriate liquidity structures for institutions within that province. The fact that actual asset structure reflects a combination of government and credit union or caisse populaire preferences is thus not a major problem. What is a problem is ceilings placed on interest rates, which in a time of rising market interest rates induce changes in portfolios between credit union deposits and deposits with other institutions.[20]

It is difficult also to discern a regional pattern of liquidity preference, because the structure of assets is determined to a considerable extent by the structure of liabilities, reflecting the particular niche in the financial system carved out by credit unions and caisses populaires in each region. Thus, for example, since around half of liabilities in the Atlantic region take the form of share capital, the proportion of assets held liquid is in the same range as in Ontario and BC with much lower share capital as a proportion of total liabilities. Quebec's liquid liability structure is reflected in a high liquid asset ratio. In the Atlantic region also, non-mortgage loans are large relative to mortgage loans, the reverse of the situation in Quebec and BC. In general, between 1976 and 1980, there was a shift from investments to more liquid assets, and from non-mortgage loans to mortgage loans. Liabilities also became more liquid in that share capital fell (except in Quebec and the Prairies) as a proportion of total liabilities. Within the deposit total there was a shift to more demand deposits relative to time deposits in the Atlantic region, and to more time deposits relative to demand deposits in Quebec and BC.

Overall, then, it is possible to see some changes in portfolio structure between 1976 and 1980 which follow the expected pattern of attempts to increase liquidity in deteriorating economic conditions, particularly in the poorer regions. But the different rôle of credit unions and caisses populaires in the different regions, combined with different legislative environments influencing relative interest rates, together make any categoric interpretation of the data very difficult.

Other financial institutions for which regional data are available are trust companies and mortgage companies, although these data have only been published since 1978. As with the chartered banks, only some balance sheet data can be allocated to specific regions (see Tables 4.33 and 4.34).[21] For both types of company, mortgage loans are by far the most significant of the regionally-specific assets. Simply comparing total selected assets and liabilities of trust companies suggests a redistribution of funds from Quebec and Ontario to the other regions, particularly the Prairies and BC. However, while the liabilities account for almost all sources of trust company funds, only fifty-eight per cent of assets are accounted for. It is not at all unlikely that a relatively high proportion of the remainder are the liabilities of nationwide corporations and financial institutions, headquartered in Ontario and Quebec. No conclusions may therefore be drawn either about the regional composition of total trust company assets or about any net redirection of funds out of Ontario and Quebec.

Mortgage company liabilities include a much higher component of national financial market borrowing, not included in the regional distribution of liabilities. The simple comparison between the total of selected assets and liabilities shown here implies a redistribution of funds to the Prairies and BC from all other regions. If the money market borrowing were allocated to Ontario and Quebec, then the degree of redistribution would be correspondingly greater.

4.7 CONCLUSION

With all the *caveats* relevant to interpreting these data, the evidence is consistent with the theory put forward in chapter two, according to which preferences on the part of households, corporations and regional financial institutions are systematically for more liquid portfolio structures the more pessimistic are expectations about the local economy. That, combined with national bankers' own expectations and thus unwillingness to lend in the region, causes capital outfows to more prosperous regions, via the financial centre. The resulting lower supply of liquidity further fortifies pessimistic expectations.

Higher interest rates in Peripheral regions can thus be interpreted as indicating persisting excess demand for credit. Low savings relative to investment may indicate a low income multiplier, while low deposits relative to loans may indicate a low bank, or money, multiplier; expenditure and asset leakages, respectively, are high. Households and corporations are less liquid than they would like to be when economic conditions deteriorate. Such a situation cannot fail to inhibit expenditure plans, further worsening the situation of the local economy. If the reaction of financial institutions is then to curtail lending, this cannot be identified from aggregate data, since the consequence is further reductions in expenditure, income, savings and deposits; comparing ratios of loans to any one of these aggregates among regions thus does not indicate anything about the regional allocation of new credit, other than suggesting how the regional pattern of the development process might influence this allocation. We can see that the banks' allocation of regionally specific assets, for example, fell for non-Western regions between 1976 and 1980, relative to Western Canadian assets.

The argument, then, that the banks promote regional convergence by redistributing savings cannot be sustained. We have found evidence of a relative shortage of credit in the Canadian Periphery relative to the Centre, compounded by the consequences of the relatively high liquidity preference in the Peripheral regions, particularly during downturns.

We turn now to consider the implications of these conclusions for the ways in which the public sector can alleviate these tendencies for regional divergence.

Footnotes

[1]   There is a vast literature which grapples with the problems involved in estimating expectations. No adequate technique has however been found (or can be expected to be found) for estimating expectations in a framework where they are not constrained to adjust in such a way as to ensure that markets are always in equilibrium states.

[2]   Cooley and LeRoy (1981) discuss fully the extent to which the identifcation problem has not been addressed in most work estimating demand for money functions.

[3]   This has been a matter for general discussion, as in Hicks (1979), and Addison *et al.* (1980 and 1984). But it has been a matter of particular concern with respect to the influence of demand on the determination of the supply of money, or credit, as in Moore and Stuttman (1984) and Myatt (1986).

[4]   The prevalence of rationing business credit in Canada is explained in Economic Council of Canada (1982a, chapter two).

[5]   The current account balance should include transfers, as well as the balance on goods and services. Government transfers are already dealt with in the public sector account, so the only missing component is personal and corporate interregional transfers. In the absence of information on these, we include them implicitly in the capital account.

[6]   They focussed the discussion at the 1973 Western Economic Opportunities Conference on capital financing and regional financial institutions. Quebec's provincial accounts were used in the unity debate with the federal government in 1979; see Tremblay (1977), Raynauld (1980).

[7]   See Benson (1978) for use of the banks' provincial data, and Ryba (1974a) for use of the accounts data.

[8]   See C.D. Howe (1977) for a discussion of alternative accounting procedures.

[9]   See 'Outline of Concepts and Methods' in Statistics Canada, 13-213.

[10]   See Economic Council of Canada (1982a, Chapter 2). Data on interest charges on loans from U.S. banks show that charges are higher the smaller the bank and the smaller the loan. See Boltz (1977) and Straszheim (1971).

[11]   See *Moody's Bond Record* for summary tables of typical bond yields by rating.

[12]   See confirming evidence in Fullerton (1979, p.16).

[13]   Smaller provinces' bonds may carry a risk premium reflecting
         lender's risk rather than borrower's risk. If issues are small and
         infrequent, the market in that province's bonds may be relatively thin
         and erratic, causing wider fluctuations in market value than for larger
         provinces' bonds.

[14]   Garvy (1959) estimates that a turnover rate of deposits of government
         securities dealers in 1959 was an incredible 135,168 (on a basis
         comparable to Table 5.16), compared with 3,588 for other securities
         brokers and dealers, and 413 for other New York City deposits.
         (Total turnover was 372 in the other six leading financial centres and
         288 elsewhere.)

[15]   The (Bryce) Royal Commission on Corporate Concentration (1978,
         pp.65-6) discusses why there are economies of scale in access to
         capital markets.

[16]   The data for U.S. corporations show quite the reverse (see Dow,
         1981, chapter 9), with the current asset ratio a negative function of
         firm size. According to our theory, this would suggest that in the US
         firms' portfolio choice is less constrained than in Canada. This
         conclusion is consistent with the argument that a segmented, unit
         banking systsem is more responsive to small business needs and with
         the observation that regional disparities in the US are declining,
         unlike those in Canada.

[17]   The following information was gathered primarily from conversations
         with bank officials.

[18]   The information is presented in terms of the regional distribution of
         each asset or liability rather than distribution of assets and liabilities
         within each region, since there is no appropriate asset or liability total
         for regions as the denominator. The national breakdown of the
         selected asset and liabilities by each type of asset and liability is
         shown in the last row of each table.

[19]   See Dow and Earl (1982, chapter 7) for a discussion of the
         relationship between banks and non bank financial intermediaries.

[20]   See Statistics Canada 61-209 for a listing of the relevant provincial
         legislation.

[21]   See footnote 18.

STATISTICAL APPENDIX

Table 4.1

<u>Annual % age Change in Real Gross Expenditure[a]</u>
<u>By Region, Selected Years[b]</u>

	1966	1970	1976	1980
Atlantic	6.1	4.0	6.4	-9.8
Quebec	6.2	2.1	7.2	0.5
Ontario	7.0	2.1	5.1	2.3
Prairies	8.5	0.5	3.4	7.1
BC	7.2	-0.1	8.4	2.5
Canada	6.9	2.5	5.7	1.4

a   Real GPE calculated from nominal GPE using GNE deflator.

b   See p.   for selection criteria.

<u>Source</u>:   Statistics Canada, 13-213 and 13-001

Table 4.2

<u>Per Capita Gross Provincial Product by Region</u>
<u>As % age of Canadian Average, Selected Years</u>

	1966	1970	1976	1980
Atlantic	59.8	64.4	61.3	57.0
Quebec	91.2	90.7	88.3	86.3
Ontario	119.0	119.4	109.2	105.1
Prairies	101.6	97.7	116.1	126.9
BC	111.5	106.5	108.3	110.1

<u>Source</u>:   Statistics Canada, 13-213 and 91-201.

Table 4.3

Total Chartered Bank Assets and Liabilities
Distribution by Region (%), 1976 and 1980

	1976		1980	
	Assets	Liabilities	Assets	Liabilities
Atlantic	6.4	5.2	5.7	5.2
Quebec	21.9	21.9	18.5	17.9
Ontario	39.2	43.1	39.4	45.3
Prairies	19.1	17.6	22.6	18.3
B.C.	13.3	12.1	13.7	13.3

Source: Bank of Canada *Review*

Table 4.4

Regionally Quantifiable* Chartered Bank Assets
and Liabilities
Distribution by Region (%), 1976 and 1980

	1976		1980	
	Assets	Liabilities	Assets	Liabilities
Atlantic	6.9	5.4	6.2	5.4
Quebec	22.2	20.5	18.4	17.3
Ontario	37.5	42.7	36.1	43.1
Prairies	19.0	18.7	25.0	19.9
B.C.	14.5	12.7	14.6	14.3

*   See Tables 4.24 and 4.27 for details.

Source: Bank of Canada *Review*

Table 4.5

Regional Share of GDP (%) Selected Years

	1966	1970	1976	1980
Atlantic	5.9	6.2	5.8	5.3
Quebec	26.4	25.6	23.9	22.9
Ontario	41.4	42.3	39.3	37.4
Prairies	17.2	16.2	19.4	21.8
B.C.	9.9	10.6	11.6	12.2

Source: Statistics Canada, 13-213.

Table 4.6

Regional Share of National Population (%), Selected Years

	1966	1970	1976	1980
Atlantic	9.9	9.6	9.5	9.3
Quebec	28.9	28.2	27.1	26.6
Ontario	34.8	35.5	35.9	35.6
Prairies	16.9	16.5	16.5	17.2
B.C.	9.3	10.0	10.7	11.1

Source: Statistics Canada, 91-201.

Table 4.7

Public Sector Surplus (+)/Deficit (-)
As % age of GPP, Selected Years

	1966	1970	1976	1980
Atlantic	-23.1	-19.2	-31.4	-40.6
Quebec	+3.1	+2.1	-5.3	-8.9
Ontario	+5.6	+4.7	+1.5	+0.7
Prairies	-4.4	-2.2	+5.9	+7.2
BC	+3.5	+5.0	+2.3	+2.1

Source: Statistics Canada 13-213.

Table 4.8

Net Exports Plus Expenditure Residual
As % age of GPP, Selected Years

	1966	1970	1976	1980
Atlantic	-33.1	-27.4	-35.4	-42.1
Quebec	3.5	7.9	-1.6	0.1
Ontario	4.3	5.3	5.7	9.9
Prairies	-2.2	1.3	1.7	10.1
BC	-7.7	-4.1	-2.1	-3.0

Source: Statistics Canada, 13-213.

Table 4.9

Savings Minus Investment Plus Residual
As % age of GPP, Selected Years

	1966	1970	1976	1980
Atlantic	-10.0	-8.2	-4.0	-1.5
Quebec	0.4	5.8	6.9	9.0
Ontario	-1.3	0.6	11.1	9.2
Prairies	2.2	3.5	-6.9	2.9
B.C.	-11.2	-9.1	-4.4	-5.1

Source: Tables 4.7 and 4.8 $(S-I+e) = -(T-G)+(X-M+e)$.

Table 4.10

Intra-Bank Capital Flows
as % of GPP, 1976 and 1980

	1976	1980
Atlantic	+8.5	+12.8
Quebec	-0.6	+3.3
Ontario	-5.0	-5.6
Prairies	+4.9	+12.5
B.C.	+3.9	+4.6

Source: Bank of Canada *Review* and Statistics Canada 13-213.

Table 4.11

Personal Savings Minus Investment*
As a % age of GPP, Selected Years

	1966	1970	1976	1980
Atlantic	-24.7	-23.3	-19.8	-19.9
Quebec	-14.6	-8.2	-11.1	-7.0
Ontario	-15.7	-12.3	-9.5	-4.6
Prairies	-17.2	-18.0	-24.0	-21.5
BC	-25.9	-21.3	-18.4	-18.9

* Private sector gross fixed capital formation plus change in inventories.

Source: Statistics Canada 13-213.

Table 4.12

Money Holdings[a] as a % age of GPP by Region,
Selected Years[b]

	1976		1980	
	DD/GPP	DD + SD/GPP	DD/GPP	DD + SD/GPP
Atlantic	10.4	33.7	8.5	41.8
Quebec	9.0	31.8	6.8	31.3
Ontario	11.2	40.2	9.0	8.5
Prairies	9.5	35.5	7.6	36.8
BC	9.2	38.8	9.8	47.0

a   DD = chequing and other demand deposits with chartered banks.
    SD = all other deposits with chartered banks.
    Both aggregates exclude deposits in foreign currencies.

b   Not available for 1966 or 1970.

Source: Bank of Canada, *Review*; Statistics Canada, 13-213.

Table 4.13

Regional Distribution of the Number of
Commercial Failures (%)
1966, 1970 and 1976[*]

	1966	1970	1976
Atlantic	1.3	1.4	1.5
Quebec	56.5	47.1	33.9
Ontario	34.0	36.9	50.1
Prairies	5.4	8.6	6.8
BC	2.8	6.0	7.7

[*]   Data series ended 1978.

Source: Statistics Canada, 61-002.

Table 4.14

Regional Distribution of Corporations[a] by Size,[b] 1976

	Small Corporation %	Large Corporation %
Atlantic	5.4	3.8
Quebec other than Northern Quebec	24.8	24.3
Northern Quebec and Northern Ontario	2.7	1.2
Ontario other than Northern Ontario	34.7	42.6
Prairies	18.7	16.9
BC	13.6	11.2

a   Location refers to location of head office.
b   Small corporations have assets of $5 million or less, all others being
     classified as large.

Source: Economic Council of Canada.

Table 4.15

Mortgage Interest Rates: % age Deviation
From Canadian Average, Selected Years

	1966			1970	1976
	Lending Institutions[a]	Other Corporations[b]	Other Lenders[c]	All NHA Approved Loans[d]	
Atlantic	+1.4	+7.9	+1.1	+0.8	+3.8
Quebec	-1.8	+36.5	-6.1	-0.2	+2.1
Ontario	-0.3	-3.2	+0.1	-0.2	-1.9
Prairies	-0.1	+2.5	-7.6	-0.1	+0.6
BC	-0.3	+23.1	+6.7	+0.9	+2.7

a   Includes life, loan and trust companies, fraternal societies and Quebec Savings Banks. Chartered banks did not commence mortgage lending until 1967.

b   Includes small loan companies, holding companies and other corporations and institutions whose mortgage lending is ancillary to their principal functions.

c   Includes credit unions, caisses populaires, pension funds, individual and other non-corporate bodies.

d   December data only. Regional data broken down by type of lender are not available for 1970 and 1976.

Source: Canadian Mortgage and Housing Corporation, *Canadian Housing Statistics*.

Table 4.16

Moody's Government Bond Ratings[a] , and Bond Yields[b]
By Province, Selected Years[c]

	1970 Rating	1970 Yield (%)	1976 Rating	1976 Yield (%)	1980 Rating	1980 Yield (%)
Atlantic						
Nova Scotia	A	9.73	A1	10.11	A1	10.88
New Brunswick	A	9.39	A1	9.17	A1	10.93
Quebec	A	9.85	Aa	9.07	Aa	11.37
Ontario	Aa	9.49	Aaa	8.80	Aaa	8.70
Prairies						
Manitoba	A	9.19	Aa	9.33	Aa	11.43
Saskatchewan	n/a	n/a	A	8.50	Aa	10.95
Alberta[d]	Aa	9.15	Aa	9.25	Aaa	n/a
B.C.[d]	Aa	n/a	Aa	7.81	Aaa	10.52
Canada	Aa	8.44	Aaa	8.63	Aaa	10.26

a   Ratings are a measure of quality, or absence of risk: Aaa, Aa, A (A1 at top of range), Baa, ...C (Aaa highest).

b   Where more than one issue outstanding, mid-point of range shown.

c   Observations taken at mid-year. Data for 1966 not available.

d   Alberta and B.C. Government utilities bonds, in absence of Provincial Government bond issues.

Source: Moody's Investor Service, *Moody's Bond Record*.

Table 4.17

Regional Share of Employment in
Finance, Insurance and Real Estate (end-year)(%),
Selected Years

	1966	1970	1976	1980
Atlantic	4.9	6.9	5.7	5.2
Quebec	28.8	28.5	25.1	23.5
Ontario	42.4	43.1	42.7	42.3
Prairies	14.4	13.3	15.7	16.7
BC	9.5	10.3	10.8	12.3

Source: Statistics Canada, 72-008.

Table 4.18

Regional Share of Branches of Banks and
Other Deposit-Taking Institutions*
Selected Years (%)

	1966 Banks	1970 Banks	1976 Banks	1976 Total	1980 Banks	1980 Total
Atlantic	7.8	7.8	7.8	7.6	8.3	7.5
Quebec	27.7	25.4	21.9	27.3	20.6	27.2
Ontario	36.0	36.9	39.1	36.9	39.0	35.9
Prairies	18.3	19.0	19.3	18.7	20.4	19.7
BC	10.2	10.9	11.9	9.5	11.7	9.7

* Credit unions, caisses populaires and trust companies; branch data not available for 1966 and 1970.

Source: Statistics Canada 61-0006 and Canadian Bankers Association, *Bank Directory of Canada*.

Table 4.19

Rate of Turnover of Chequing Deposits, By Region, Selected Years[*]

| | 1976 | | | 1980 | | | |
	$\frac{CC}{D1}$	$\frac{CC}{D2}$	$\frac{CC}{D3}$	$\frac{CC}{D1}$	$\frac{CC}{D2}$	$\frac{CC}{D3}$	$\frac{CC}{D4}$
Atlantic	73.5	72.0	72.0	75.1	72.4	72.4	70.8
Quebec	145.0	97.5	85.2	221.2	133.0	108.1	107.1
Ontario	164.1	161.6	156.0	428.1	416.0	390.3	357.6
Prairies	103.6	94.1	76.7	141.6	128.0	95.9	93.7
B.C.	94.2	88.5	88.5	125.8	113.1	113.1	108.7

CC =   cheque cashings for 51 centres over 12 month period, adjusted upward by the percentage under-coverage of the survey as estimated by Statistics Canada.

D1 =   chequing deposits (demand and savings) with chartered banks.

D2 =   D1 plus chequing deposits with credit unions and caisses populaires.

D3 =   D2 plus deposits with Montreal City and District Savings Bank, Ontario Savings Offices and Alberta Treasury Branches (chequing/non-chequing breakdown not available)

D4 =   D3 plus chequing deposits with mortgage companies and trust companies (not available for 1976)

*   Data not available for 1966 and 1970.

Source: Statistics Canada 61-001 and 61-006, Bank of Canada *Review*, and Annual Reports of the Institutions included in D3.

Table 4.20

Personal Demand Deposits and Savings Deposits With
Chartered Banks, Regional Distribution (%) Selected Years*

	1976		1980	
	Personal Demand Deposits	Personal Savings Deposits	Personal Demand Deposits	Personal Savings Deposits
Atlantic	6.3	6.2	6.6	6.1
Quebec	11.1	18.2	11.1	15.7
Ontario	38.8	42.5	36.2	43.3
Prairies	26.3	19.4	28.6	19.7
B.C.17.5	13.7	17.6	15.2	
Total	100.0	100.0	100.0	100.0

* Not available for 1966 and 1970.

Source: Bank of Canada, *Review*.

Table 4.21

Distribution of Unearned Household Income (%)
By Source of Income and Region, Selected Years*

	1976				1980			
	Bank Interest	Bond Interest	Net Dividends	Cap. Gains	Bank Interest	Bond Interest	Net Dividends	Cap. Gains
Atlantic	54.8	13.4	24.6	7.2	49.5	9.5	27.0	14.0
Quebec	55.9	17.0	17.6	9.5	52.5	11.9	18.4	17.1
Ontario	55.7	13.7	21.5	9.5	45.6	8.6	27.8	18.0
Prairies	45.0	11.1	12.7	31.2	37.9	5.5	24.4	32.2
BC	46.6	13.6	20.1	19.7	36.5	6.2	24.7	32.6

* Net capital gain component not available for 1966 and 1970.

Source: Revenue Canada Taxation.

Table 4.22

Composition of Household* Financial Assets (%)
By Region, Selected Years

	1970				1977			
		Total				Total		
	Depos-its	Bonds	Liquid Assets	Stocks	Depos-its	Bonds	Liquid Assets	Stocks
Atlantic	36.3	26.8	66.0	15.4	64.4	13.1	80.2	5.0
Quebec	47.9	23.1	73.0	15.4	56.2	17.8	75.7	3.8
Ontario	40.6	19.1	61.0	16.1	50.0	15.1	65.8	12.7
Prairies	47.2	24.1	72.7	16.2	57.8	15.2	74.1	5.7
BC	41.4	14.6	57.0	23.3	30.9	9.9	41.5	5.7

* Families and unattached individuals

Source: Statistics Canada, 13-547 for Spring 1970 survey and Statistics Canada, 13-572 for Spring 1977 survey.

Table 4.23

Ratios of Current Assets to Current Liabilities,
(Interval Location of Median[a])
by Region and Size of Corporation,[b] 1976

	Small Corp.	Large Corp.
Atlantic	4.01	4.26
Quebec other than Northern Quebec	4.60	4.84
Northern Quebec and Northern Ontario	4.13	4.40
Ontario other than Northern Ontario	4.64	5.83
Prairies	4.32	4.57
BC	3.94	4.36

a The data are provided in frequency distribution form, with twelve intervals. On the simplifying assumption that the distribution is linear within each interval, a value of 4.01, for example, signifies that the median observation is one per cent into the fifth interval, 4.26 signifies 26% into the fifth interval, and so on.
b Small corporations have assets of $5 million or less, all others being classified as large.

Source: Economic Council of Canada.

Table 4.24

Ratio of Short Term Bank Loans to assets
(Interval Location of Median[a])
by Region and Size of Corporation,[b] 1976

	Small Corp.	Large Corp.
Atlantic	3.80	4.40
Quebec other than Northern Quebec	2.98	2.91
Northern Quebec and Northern Ontario	3.54	2.25
Ontario other than Northern Ontario	2.14	1.99
Prairies	2.04	1.83
BC	1.00	2.34

a,b. See footnotes, Table 4.23.

Source: Economic Council of Canada

Table 4.25

Selected[a] Chartered Bank Assets[b]
Distribution by Region[c] (%), 1976

	Personal Loans	Bus. Loans Under $0.2M	Other Bus. Loans	Agric. Loans to Farmers	Prov./ Munic. Loans & Secur- ities	Residence Mortgage Loans	Total
Atlantic	10.1	7.4	5.6	2.2	10.3	3.7	6.9
Quebec	18.6	21.6	25.1	4.7	47.2	19.6	22.2
Ontario	37.3	36.5	41.1	28.3	24.4	37.8	37.5
Prairies	18.0	14.9	16.1	57.5	11.0	19.6	19.0
BC	16.0	19.5	12.2	7.4	7.1	19.3	14.5
Total[d]	28.5	9.9	36.2	5.3	5.4	14.7	100.0

a   Selected according to amenability to regional allocation.
b   Accounts for 66.9% of total assets.
c   First five rows show the share of each asset held in each region, each
    column of five shares adding to 100% (except for rounding error).
d   Total row refers to the share of each asset item for all regions, adding
    across to 100% (except for rounding error).
Source: Bank of Canada, *Review*.

Table 4.26

Selected[a] Chartered Bank Assets[b]
Distribution by Region[c] (%), 1980

	Personal Loans	Bus. Loans Under $0.2M	Other Bus. Loans	Agric. Loans to Farmers	Prov./ Munic. Loans & Secur- ities	Residence Mortgage Loans	Total
Atlantic	11.0	6.6	4.6	1.7	13.7	4.6	6.2
Quebec	19.5	20.4	17.5	8.6	53.3	16.4	18.4
Ontario	35.2	34.2	38.1	31.8	16.5	37.5	36.1
Prairies	18.9	19.5	27.6	48.5	8.9	22.1	25.0
BC	15.4	19.4	12.2	9.4	7.5	19.5	14.6
Total[d]	20.2	9.5	42.0	6.9	2.8	18.8	100.0

a   See footnote a, Table 4.25.
b   Accounts for 59.3% of total assets
c   See footnote c, Table 4.25
d   See footnote d, Table 4.25.
Source: Bank of Canada, *Review*.

Table 4.27

Selected[a] Chartered Bank Liabilities[b]
Distribution[c] by Region (%), 1976

	Personal Demand Deposits	Other Demand Deposits	Personal Savings Deposits	Other Notice Deposits	Total
Atlantic	6.3	5.4	6.2	3.3	5.4
Quebec	11.1	21.6	18.2	26.4	20.5
Ontario	38.8	41.7	42.5	44.6	42.7
Prairies	26.3	19.3	19.4	15.6	18.7
BC	17.5	6.1	13.7	10.1	12.7
Total[d]	4.0	15.0	56.5	24.4	100.0

a See footnote a, Table 4.25
b Accounts for 56.7% of total liabilities
c See footnote c, Table 4.25
d See footnote d, Table 4.25.

Source: Bank of Canada, *Review*

Table 4.28

Selected[a] Chartered Bank Liabilities[b]
Distribution[c] by Region (%), 1980

	Personal Demand Deposits	Other Demand Deposits	Personal Savings Deposits	Other Notice Deposits	Total
Atlantic	6.6	5.9	6.1	3.5	5.4
Quebec	11.1	18.5	15.7	21.2	17.3
Ontario	36.2	34.6	43.3	46.7	43.1
Prairies	28.6	25.4	19.7	17.3	19.9
BC	17.6	15.7	15.2	11.3	14.3
Total[d]	3.2	9.9	60.1	26.7	100.0

a See footnote a, Table 4.25
b Accounts for 46.0% of total liabilities
c See footnote c, Table 4.25
d See footnote d, Table 4.25.

Source: Bank of Canada, *Review*

Table 4.29

Composition of Assets* of Local Credit Unions
and Caisses Populaires (%) by Region, 1976

	Cash & Demand Deposits	Investments	Non-Mortgage Loans	Mortgage Loans
Atlantic	5.7	10.4	64.8	15.3
Quebec	23.6	10.7	21.2	41.4
Ontario	4.9	13.2	48.3	30.3
Prairies	2.8	20.1	32.0	35.1
BC	4.8	10.4	13.1	68.0

*   Data refer to the percentage of total assets in that region devoted to
     each type of asset.

Source: Statistics Canada, 61-006.

Table 4.30

Composition of Assets* of Local Credit Unions
and Caisses Populaires (%) by Region, 1980

	Cash & Demand Deposits	Investments	Non-Mortgage Loans	Mortgage Loans
Atlantic	6.9	9.4	61.1	18.7
Quebec	16.5	6.8	21.8	52.0
Ontario	9.0	11.4	36.1	39.5
Prairies	2.6	17.1	32.3	43.8
BC	2.0	16.3	11.0	66.8

*   See footnote, Table 4.28

Source: Statistics Canada, 61-006.

Table 4.31

Composition of Liabilities* of Local Credit Unions
and Caisses Populaires (%) by Region, 1976

	Demand Deposits	Time Deposits	Share Capital	Loans
Atlantic	11.0	27.6	50.6	3.8
Quebec	52.7	31.3	10.0	0.5
Ontario	35.3	19.2	37.3	2.6
Prairies	36.4	38.4	17.0	3.7
BC	33.4	47.6	11.1	2.6

*   Data refer to the percentage of total liabilities in that region devoted
to each type of liability.

Source: Statistics Canada, 61-006.

Table 4.32

Composition of Liabilities* of Local Credit Unions
and Caisses Populaires (%) by Region, 1980

	Demand Deposits	Time Deposits	Share Capital	Loans
Atlantic	21.1	27.6	42.4	3.8
Quebec	45.1	36.6	10.2	2.1
Ontario	47.1	26.2	20.9	1.9
Prairies	42.0	42.0	8.8	3.8
BC	30.5	58.6	4.0	2.4

*   See footnote, Table 4.31

Source: Statistics Canada, 61-006.

Table 4.33

Selected[a] Trust Company Assets and Liabilities[b]
Distribution by Region[c] (%) 1980

	Assets				Liabilities			
	Short Term Invsmts	Long Term Invsmts	Mort- gage Loans	Per- sonal Loans	Total	Demand Depos- its	Term Depos- its	Total
Atlantic	6.9	4.9	6.5	5.9	6.4	4.6	6.5	5.9
Quebec	41.5	45.7	9.0	3.6	10.0	9.2	13.2	12.3
Ontario	13.5	36.3	50.0	62.0	50.1	63.0	56.3	57.9
Prairies	38.2	9.3	23.9	17.4	23.2	14.5	16.9	16.4
BC	0.0	3.8	11.4	11.2	11.1	8.6	7.3	7.6
Total[d]	0.2	3.1	92.2	4.5	100.0	22.9	77.1	100.0

a   See footnote a, Table 4.25
b. Accounts for 57.7% of total assets and 93.2% of total liabilities
c   See Footnote c, Table 4.25
d   See Footnote d, Table 4.25.
Source: Statistics Canada, 61-006.

Table 4.34

Selected[a] MortgageCompany Assets and Liabilities[b]
Distribution by Region[c] (%) 1980

	Assets				Liabilities			
	Short Term Invsmts	Long Term Invsmts	Mort- gage Loans	Per- sonal Loans	Total	Demand Depos- its	Term Depos- its	Total
Atlantic	10.0	8.5	7.4	4.0	7.4	4.5	9.5	9.2
Quebec	52.0	29.2	15.4	0.3	15.3	7.5	17.4	16.7
Ontario	38.6	50.5	35.6	49.0	35.7	55.9	40.9	41.9
Prairies	0.0	4.6	23.4	17.0	23.3	18.3	20.7	20.5
BC	0.0	3.0	18.1	25.8	18.1	13.9	11.4	11.6
Total[d]	0.1	0.3	92.2	0.6	100.0	6.4	93.6	100.0

a   See footnote a, Table 4.25
b   Accounts for 88.9% of total assets and 66.2% of total liabilities
c   See Footnote c, Table 4.25
d   See Footnote d, Table 4.25.
Source: Statistics Canada, 61-006.

5 Policy implications

5.1 INTRODUCTION

The primary purpose of the theoretical discussion in chapter two was to provide an economic explanation for the financial interrelationships among Canada's regions described in chapter three. This explanation rested on the potentially destabilising rôle of market forces in an environment of unequal economic and financial development. As such it was juxtaposed with the customary political explanations which rely either on the capricious prejudices of bankers, or else on the unreasonable demands of residents of low productivity regions. The explanation was also juxtaposed with orthodox economic theory which envisages financial interrelationships between regions as being stabilising, if of significance at all. The evidence in chapter four, provides confirmation for our alternative theory of financial instability.

To the extent that the discussion so far promotes a better understanding of regional financial interrelationships, that in itself would represent progress. But the discussion can be taken further by considering the implications of that understanding for policy issues, particularly in the area of regional policy. It is of fundamental importance to the aims and conduct of regional policy how one understands the process of regional development. In particular, it is important whether private sector activity is viewed as promoting regional convergence or divergence. The state has throughout Canada's history played a central rôle in directing the pattern of regional development. But the rôle of the state in influencing the future pattern of development of regions now well-established warrants general consideration, which we provide here in the next section.

While it has been argued here that financial markets contribute, on balance, to regional divergence, this contribution is seen as only part of a systemic process which is not at all independent of real economic conditions in the different regions. Thus the behaviour of financial markets will be influenced by perceptions of these conditions, and how they are affected by regional policy in general. But the rôle of the state vis-a-vis financial institutions warrants particular consideration, because the activities of financial markets are defined by the regulatory framework and because confidence in the system derives from confidence in the state's regulatory powers and also in its liabilities, which underpin the financial system. It has been one of the aims here to demonstrate the importance of the regional dimension of the national financial system; there is a direct corollary that the conduct of monetary policy and the regulatory framework also have regional dimensions, which we consider in turn in sections three and four.

5.2 REGIONAL POLICY IN GENERAL: ITS PURPOSE AND RATIONALE

It is a reasonable characterisation that Canada's federal government includes in its goals high national levels of employment and income, and a distribution of those levels which is equitable among persons and between regions. The goal of promoting all regions' employment and income levels is reinforced by the federal structure of government in Canada, whereby the interests of the provinces are represented by the provincial governments which themselves have not inconsiderable powers in the policy arena, although differing degrees of economic and political power.

It is an important policy issue in itself how far the goals with respect to national variables conflict with goals as to their regional distribution. Is regional equity only pursued at the cost of national efficiency? Even if not, can the improvement of one region's lot only be achieved at the cost of deterioration of other regions' positions? The Macdonald Commission (Government of Canada, 1985, p.199) reaffirmed regional goals for the federal government, but expressed these as involving a trade-off with national efficiency.

According to orthodox economic theory, there may be a trade off between equity and efficiency in the short-run, but not in the long-run, if wages and prices are fully flexible. Even if labour and capital are immobile between regions, trade in goods and services between regions will (under strict conditions) equalise real incomes across regions. (See Samuelson 1949). This result requires each region to specialise in the industry in which it has comparative advantage as determined by its endowment of factors. Any short-run deviation of prices of goods or factors from the national norm would result in trade imbalances, deficits in regions with excessively high wages and prices, surpluses elsewhere. The resulting monetary outflow from the deficit regions to the surplus regions would cause wages and prices to fall in the former and rise in the latter, restoring them to nationwide equality. (See Courchene 1978.)

The adjustment process is further facilitated if labour and capital are mobile between regions. Then industrial specialisation is determined by natural resource endowment, and labour and capital move to regions where the return is highest. Factor inflows serve to equalise factor returns directly just as trade flows equalise prices. In this case regional equity refers to equality of per capita income, where each region's population is determined by the productivity of the natural resource endowment. Should that productivity fall in one region, population must also fall to maintain income equality. Except under certain conditions, including the possibility of migration being costly, the efficient national outcome is again that which equalises factor incomes.[1]

Government policy designed to promote equality of regional per capita income should, according to this approach, be geared to reinforcing the adjustment process, promoting wage and price flexibility, and labour and capital mobility. 'Capital' is generally used to refer to financial and physical capital interchangeably in this context, and therefore capital mobility includes the mobility of funds within the financial system, seeking out the highest returns. Further, the initial factor endowments can be improved in low-productivity regions by facilitating the acquisition of skills. As a corollary, any other government policy designed to equalise incomes in the short-run will simply prevent market forces from equalising incomes in the long-run. While setting out these arguments Courchene (1978, 1981, 1986) also incorporates an analysis of the monetary aspects of adjustment along the lines of the gold standard adjustment process referred to above. While others (Kaldor 1970, for example) have welcomed the stabilising regional effect of fiscal stabilisers, Courchene argues that the inflow of federal transfers to a region in trade deficit prevents the automatic adjustment to wages and prices which would have resulted from the original monetary outflow.

While labour mobility may be seen at the national level as a useful part of the regional adjustment process, it is not necessarily welcome at the regional level. For a region such as the Atlantic region, with a consistently high unemployment rate, a steady population drain may be unacceptable to the provincial governments for reasons of their relative standing within confederation, and to the local population whose goals may include preserving a particular lifestyle in familiar surroundings, as much as increasing income. Indeed, depopulation of large areas of the country is not popularly regarded as an acceptable solution to regional disparities any more than would depopulation of Canada to reduce income disparities between Canada and the US. Labour mobility is more acceptable to recipient provinces, although social costs are incurred, including congestion and social instability, particularly if the migration is cyclical. Indeed there is concern that migration may be destabilising rather than stabilising in an economic sense also, because of the damaging effect of out-migration on the local availability of skilled labor and on local effective demand. (See Polese, 1981.)

An efficiency argument for regional equity without significant migration has been developed in terms of the trade-off between wage inflation and unemployment (the short-run Phillips curve). Lipsey (1960) and Archibald (1969) have explored the possibility that low degrees of regional unemployment disparity are associated with more favourable trade-offs between inflation and unemployment at the national level. As a more general phenomenon, an association has been observed in international comparisons between higher incomes and lower degrees of regional disparity (beyond the early stages of economic development). (See Williamson, 1965.)

The rationale for suggesting that it is greater regional equality which *causes* a more favourables national trade-off (rather than vice versa, or a third, common cause) is not always well specified. One rationale is as follows: Wages in low-productivity regions are influenced by wages elsewhere; the greater the disparity in productivity, the more excessive will be wages in the low-productivity regions and the higher will be unemployment. By steering towards the high-unemployment region those industries which can use the available skills or provide retraining, the less will be the regional disparity in productivity and in labour market power. More slack in the low unemployment region will dampen future wage demands which in turn will be less out of line with the new labour market situation in the former high unemployment region. A national expansion of employment will have less impact on wage inflation. The evidence for the Canadian economy does not in fact provide much support for the theory (see Kaliski, 1972 and Thirsk, 1973), although Higgins (1975) and Hewings (1978) express doubts about the appropriateness of the testing procedure. In any case, however, the Phillips curve argument could be translated into a standard orthodox argument that equity and efficiency are both served by increasing the responsiveness of labor markets, particularly if labour is not mobile.

Alternatively, the Phillips curve argument could be seen as one aspect of the theory that regional disparities are the outcome of a process of cumulative causation which exaggerates some initial, minor, disparity. If market forces act to destabilise regional economic relationships causing waste of human and capital resources, then any attempt by government to counteract those forces can increase national well-being at the same time as minimising regional disparities.

The concept of efficiency generally connotes maximised utility given the constraints of factor endowments and production possibilities. Within neoclassical theory it is a static, real, concept in the sense of involving a single configuration of output and relative prices which is most efficient. If however the motivating force of economic agents is financial accumulation, then the most efficient configuration of economic activity is that which allows the greatest value increases for asset holders. Efficiency in this sense is promoted by concentration of activity yielding monopoly or oligopoly profits, concentraton in financial markets allowing speculative capital gains, and less than full employment allowing cheap labour inputs.[2] The outcome of market forces within such a framework uses resources inefficiently in three ways: human resources are unemployed through labour market rationing rather than voluntary leisure-seeking; physical capital (as distinct from financial capital) is not generally mobile and is unemployed when activity is reduced in a particular region; within concentrated product markets demand for many goods becomes endogenous, the product of marketing, while basic needs go unmet due to lack of ability to pay.

While the location of natural resources at one time governed the location of economic activity, the shift of activity into the manufacturing and service sectors diminishes that spatial link. (See Kaldor, 1970.) In other words, there is no natural law by which the accumulation process is concentrated in a particular location. Certainly, Ontario's early prosperity can be explained by the productivity of its agricultural base, relative to Quebec. (See McCallum, 1980, Sitwell and Seifreid, 1984.) Its continued relative prosperity, however, can be explained additionally by the returns on the accumulation of assets arising from that early agricultural prosperity, assets not located necessarily in Ontario. An important contributing factor in managing that accumulation was the location in Toronto of the head offices of major financial institutions. The most important locational factor now for production is proximity to markets, which provides a self-fulfilling rationale for continued spatial concentration. Correspondingly, a successful regional policy which promoted more balanced regional growth of economic activity would automatically promote greater regional diffusion of markets. The question of economies of scale, which would suggest benefits attached to concentration of markets, must in the Canadian context be considered in terms of the entire North American market. Thus, while population growth in the Maritimes, for example, could conceivably not be great enough to support some manufacturing industry on the strength of the local market, a wider market would be available in the North-Eastern part of the United States. Economies of scale will always require concentration of some heavy industry, but the new light manufacturing industries can more successfully be regionally dispersed.

The Canadian economy is still dependent to a considerable degree on the natural resource sector, with worldwide markets beyond Canadian governmental control. Cyclical downturns in world demand for particular natural resources are a frequent starting point for a stagnation phase in regional economies. Once regional assets within that sector are devalued as a result of reduced demand, the ball is set rolling for expectations of downward adjustments to other asset prices, and the resulting reduced willingness to provide credit, and capital outflows. This process is not easily reversed when export demand picks up again, given a diminished work force and a deteriorating physical capital stock, combined with strengthened views as to the riskiness of local financial assets.

Given the costs attached to movements out and in of labour and capital, government regional policy has a rôle in providing income, employment and basic services during downturns to smooth out cycles. Addressing the source of the problem, policy can usefully be geared to promoting a new balanced industrial structure which would reduce the vulnerability of resource-dependent regions in the long term. Not simply a matter of picking up cyclical economic slack, such a strategy can reduce the degree to which the demand-deficiency in one sector generates pessimistic expectations about all asset prices. If the government can successfully convey its commitment to stabilising a region's economy, then perceptions of risk will be modified, allowing a self-fulfilling confidence in the region.

Where regional unemployment rises because of a cyclical contraction in demand originating within Canada, conventional fiscal tools may be applied to stabilise the national economy. Indeed the automatic fiscal stabilisers of rising expenditure and falling taxation during downturns are also automatic regional stabilisers in that they have most impact where the downturn is most severe. Beyond that, the question of regional fiscal policy is complicated for Canada by the federal-provincial structure of government. Thus a discretionary regional fiscal policy implemented by the federal government is politically

127

difficult given the implications of favouring some regions at the expense of others. The closest approximation is the system of equalisation payments to provincial governments with a below average tax base which allows transfers to finance the provision of basic services.[3] Indeed regional stabilisation policy as a means of dampening the effects of different cyclical patterns in different regions is justified by the Economic Council of Canada (1977) and by the Macdonald Commission (Royal Commission on the Economic Union and Development Prospects for Canada, 1985; see also Mansell and Copithorne, 1986 and Vanderkamp, 1986.)

In fact, it can be shown that the regional composition of federal revenues and expenditures affects not only the regional composition of income, but also the national level, depending on the marginal propensities to save and import in the different regions. Using regional income multiplier analysis, Miller (1980) and Miller and Wallace (1982) show that national fiscal policy can in fact be made more effective by tailoring its regional composition to reflect the areas of worst unemployment in the case of expansionary policy, or of inflation in the case of contractionary policy. Focusing an increase in spending on the Maritimes, for example, when central Canada's unemployment rate is not very high, will have spillover effects in central Canada as a result of import leakages, but a much higher proportion of the multiplied injection will still remain in the Maritimes than if the initial injection had occurred in central Canada.

Financial constraints on a region's expansion only become significant during the supermultiplier process, whereby the multiplied income increase induces new investment which starts off a further income-multiplier process.[4] Unless firms have sufficient retained earnings, new investment requires new finance whose availability is determined to a large extent by the perception of risk attached to the project and to the local economy. If the increase in government expenditure were financed by new money, and if the expansion generated sufficient optimism in the local economy, then the new money would have been retained in the local economy and be available as reserves against expanded credit. However, if pessimism persists in spite of the injection of funds, the unwillingness to embark on new investment projects will be mirrored by an absence of available finance. Government expenditures thus automatically increase local liquidity in the expenditure location, but how far this is made available to finance further expansion depends on expectations as to the value of local assets. While saving and import leakages from the income multiplier are relatively stable, leakages from the credit creation process are more capricious. The actual redistributive effect of the composition of federal government expenditure depends as much on the bank multiplier applied to the funds spent as on the income multiplier applied to the income generated.[5]

Because of the political difficulties faced by the federal government in engaging in overt discrimination between regions in its fiscal policy, most discussion has centred round fiscal policy as practised by the provincial governments.[6] While the Economic Council of Canada (1982) and Fortin (1982) note that the provinces have generally kept their budgets stable over the cycle, there is scope for more active fiscal policy attuned to each province's economic situation. The major constraint is seen as being limited access to funds to finance a deficit, given the federal government's control over money creation. Auld (1978) argues in favour of controlled provincial government access to new money financing, since otherwise borrowing would potentially be in conflict with national monetary and exchange rate policy. Recognising the disadvantaged position from which the provinces borrow in domestic markets, relative to the federal government, the Economic Council of Canada (1982a) suggests that borrowing privileges might be established up to some limit at federal interest rates. The Council does however conclude that such an arrangement would cause too many difficulties for a limited return, given that the provinces do not actually engage in active countercyclical fiscal policy.

However a provincial deficit were financed, a matter which Barber (1966) does not envisage as causing serious problems, given the magnitudes involved, the inflow of funds to the provincial economy adds fuel to the expansionary effect of increased expenditure. Since most provincial borrowing is from outside the province, the inflow of funds made available to a provincial government (with low perceived risk of default) would serve to reverse the outflow of capital from declining provinces. Once in the provincial financial system, some additional new finance would be made available for local borrowers who had been the subject of rationing. To the extent that the money enters the banking system, however, and the banks' perceptions of credit-worthiness have not altered, the funds can easily disappear from the provincial economy. The financial aspects of regional fiscal policy thus depend crucially on the structure of the financial system.

The main planks of regional policy suggested so far involve increasing aggregate demand in demand-deficient regions, and injecting confidence in the future value of local assets in order to encourage new physical investment and the retention of new money in the region to finance that investmesnt. But money creation and the financial structure themselves are under government influence, if not control. In the next two sections, we explore these two aspects of government policy for further means to inhibit the destabilising power of financial institutions.

5.3 THE REGIONAL IMPACT OF MONETARY POLICY

Legal tender, in the form of notes and coin, is a liability of the Bank of Canada. In addition, the federal government issues Treasury bills and bonds which are important assets in the financial system, bearing effectively no default risk, and being traded generally in active markets. The Bank of Canada through its monetary policy and the federal government in its borrowing policy influence the volume of legal tender, Treasury bills and federal bonds available to the public, and thus (in the absence of institutional change) the maximum capacity of the domestic financial system to generate credit.

As we discussed in chapter two, while the banking system now provides the impetus for deposit and credit creation, it is still subject to the influence of the central bank, as the issuer of one form of outside money, and as a major actor in financial markets.

The first question to be addressed is whether monetary policy in general has a differential regional impact, or whether it is regionally neutral. The second question is whether, given the existing structure of private sector financial institutions, monetary policy could be designed in such a way as to reduce regional disparities.

Most of the work by economists on the regional impact of monetary policy has referred exclusively to the United States.[7] The US banking systsem is made up of some 14,000 unit banks grouped into tiers by a correspondent banking system, and connected to the Federal Reserve Board by their supervision by one of the twelve Federal Reserve District Banks. An important question for the US is how quickly and effectively an open market purchase or sale of bonds in New York is transmitted to all the other banks. It has no direct relevance for the Canadian banking system, however, given that all ten banks have head offices or trading offices in Toronto. The American studies do, however, have indirect relevance in demonstrating the high degree of capital mobility within a national banking system even when that nation is large and there are some 14,000 banks.

More directly relevant are those studies which analyse the effect of a particular monetary policy change, once transmitted to all regions, on regions with different economic strcutures. Fishkind (1977), for example, shows that some US states consistently have more severe downturns than others. He explains this in terms of the different interest elasticity of expenditure in each state, depending on its economic structure. The construction and consumer durable industries, for example, are hit on both the demand and supply sides by high interest rates resulting from tight monetary policy imposed at the peak of the cycle. Those states particularly dependent on such sectors, he argues, should be compensated by fiscal transfers.

In Canada also there are significant differences in the strength of regional cycles, particularly in the downturn phase, although the timing is similar in all regions.[8] Certainly the regions identified by the Economic Council of Canada (1968) as experiencing the most severe cyclical increases in unemployment, the Atlantic region, Quebec and BC, are the major producers of materials employed by the construction industry.

In fact the regional pattern in credit squeezes in Canada has generally been perceived as deriving from the regional size distribution of corporations. Thus, for example, the four Western provinces' submission to the Western Economic Opportunities Conference in 1973[9] argued that small business loans are marginal to banks and thus the first to be cut back when credit is restricted; a region such as the West with a relatively high incidence of small business is thus hit harder by tight monetary policy. (The Prairies do not appear to have particularly severe downturns in terms of unemployment rates, but the deteriorating employment position during downturns is often disguised by high rates of out-migration.)

The Economic Council of Canada (1968) claims that the evidence for such an argument is not convincing. Young and Helliwell's (1964) study for the Porter Commission, based on questionnaire evidence, does however suggest that there is a higher incidence of postponements of investment among smaller firms outside of Ontario and Quebec during periods of tight monetary policy. While the Atlantic region seemed to be an exception, this was explained by the relative lack of large investment projects available for postponement.[10] Further, a more recent Economic Council of Canada (1982b) study explicitly acknowledges the marginality to banks of loans to small and medium-sized businesses, particularly in remote areas, arguing that they are the victims of quantity rationing rather than price rationing.

Even if monetary policy were neutral in its effects on different sectors and on different types and locations of business, and thus on different regions, there would still be a regional dimension in terms of whether or not monetary policy should in fact be regionally neutral anyway. If, quite apart from financial considerations, the Atlantic region's unemployment rate is unacceptably high at all stages of the cycle then, as Passaris (1975, 1976, 1977) suggests, the region should be shielded from tight monetary policy aimed at dampening expansion occurring elsewhere. As Gaskin (1960) argues, a region which has experienced low growth even during an upswing will have its chances of maintaining even that growth rate diminished if existing firms have only restricted access to working capital and new firms to start-up funds.

Before considering proposals for regionally differentiated monetary policy, it is worthwhile to consider in more detail the means by which a successfully tight monetary policy instigated by the Bank of Canada becomes translated into reduced credit availability for particular borrowers. The Bank of Canada can influence the money supply (notes and coin plus bank deposits) either by determining the amount of bank reserves in the system (since deposits can only grow up to a maximum multiple of reserves) or by determining the cost of new reserves; the former involves determining supply, the latter demand.

Both methods involve a rise in interest rates when the Bank of Canada attempts to reduce the growth of money holdings.

These attempts may fail for two primary reasons. First, if demand for credit is strong because of rising anticipated returns from investment, borrowers will be prepared to pay the higher loan charges necessitated by the higher cost of reserves. As long as the Bank of Canada acts as a lender of last resort, it is impossible to control directly the supply of reserves, and thus of total deposits. Second, the Canadian economy is open to international capital flows which respond particularly to international interest rate differentials (adjusted for expected exchange rate movements). Since the Canadian dollar is floating, theoretically a relative rise in interest rates, during a credit squeeze which attracts capital inflows, should cause the exchange rate to rise, discouraging further inflows; the effect on the domestic money supply is minimal. But if speculators expect the exchange rate to continue to rise, capital inflows will persist. If the Bank of Canada wants to prevent what it sees as an excessive exchange rate appreciation, it will buy up the excess supply of foreign exchange with new money, and the money supply will rise. The fact that the Bank's foreign exchange reserves do fluctuate indicates that there is some intervention in the foreign exchange market, with a direct effect on the domestic money supply. Thus, when foreign wealth holders share domestic expectations of capital gains and the Bank of Canada attempts to hold the dollar down, credit can be increased by foreign borrowing.

Finally, even if the Bank of Canada could always control the volume of bank deposits this may not have the desired effect on economic activity. Monetary tightness is normally introduced to dampen aggregate demand during an inflationary boom (although in recent years it has been used to dampen an inflationary recession). Financial systems in an expansionary phase are however adept at innovating either to allow more efficient use of existing money or to generate new forms of money or sources or of credit, especially those issued by non-bank financial intermediaries.[11]

In the US, it is possible to analyse the regional impact of monetary policy by looking not only at the different expenditure effects of interest rate changes, but also at the different portfolio behaviour of financial institutions in different regions; given an equi-proportional fall in reserves in all banks, by how much is local credit reduced in each region?[12] In Canada, there is no *necessary* relationship between reserves of each bank and its assets in a particular region. Yet each branch does act as a profit centre so that it can be analysed in a similar way to an American unit bank, with imputed profits lower the greater the leakage of deposits to other regions from a given creation of credit in the same way that bank multipliers are lower the higher the rate of leakage out of reserves.

Suppose the Bank of Canada increased Bank Rate in order to reduce monetary growth because an expansion in Central Canada is becoming inflationary. Banks increase their lending rates in line with the rising cost of new reserves. Demand for loans is discouraged where there is no change in expected returns on investment, so that marginal projects are no longer viable. If the boom is well-established in Central Canada, however, expected returns, particularly in highly speculative markets like real estate, will be rising anyway so that loan demand will not be discouraged. So long as borrowers in less prosperous regions are perceived as having higher default risk than Central Canadian borrowers, the rising demand among the latter will be met by quantity rationing among the former. As the Economic Council of Canada (1982b) points out, rationing is most prevalent among small and medium-sized businesses, especially in remote areas, even though they may actually be no more risk-prone than large, well-established corporations.[13]

The preference for large corporations and familiarity with corporate borrowers is even more significant in foreign borrowing, so that even when large corporations are denied credit domestically, they are more likely to have access to foreign credit. So, even if the Bank of Canada does not intervene to prevent the rise of the dollar, the composition of credit represented by the given money supply will have shifted in favour of large borrowers with an established reputation in international markets.

Finally, financial innovations spread from the financial centre out, so that new ways of economising on credit, and new money-substitutes, induced by the monetary squeeze, will allow borrowers in Central Canada to proceed with expenditure plans more easily than elsewhere. The Bank of Canada must increase Bank Rate further to enforce its tight monetary policy.

In Central Canada, other loans and thus desposits will continue to grow apace, while both will be limited in the rest of Canada. Further, rising liquidity preference in the rest of Canada as expenditure is cut back, combined with rising returns on financial assets in the financial centre (due to financial innovation and the continuing expectation of capital gains) encourage outflows of funds to the financial centre; the rate of deposit leakage from Peripheral bank branches is thus increased. The weakened profit position of these branches will induce even greater caution in lending, limiting the growth of deposits. In extreme cases, such branches may be closed down completely.

The profitability of branches (as of unit banks) is greater, the larger their portfolio is, i.e. (other things being equal) the larger the bank multiplier. But the multiplier coefficients (the rate of leakage or outflow) are not independent of the initial injection of new credit (or reserves in the case of a unit bank). If the banks were to allocate new credit in favour of small business in a remote area rather than large corporations in the Centre, this demonstration of confidence in the local economy would dampen the tendency towards increased liquidity preference with resulting outflows of funds. Earlier we touched on the multiplier analysis of regional fiscal policy. In the case of money multipliers, different regional allocations of new credit similarly have different regional effects in spite of leakage or spillover effects, and indeed have different national effects. This result is even stronger in the case of bank multipliers because the leakage rates are endogenous, reinforcing the redistributive effect of different credit allocations. (See Dow, 1982.)

Just as the case can be made, given significant regional differences in unemployment rate, for a regionally differentiated fiscal policy to focus expansion or contraction where it is most appropriate, a similar case can be made for a regionally differentiated monetary policy. The possibility of a regional element in monetary policy is raised periodically in policy discussions, and was indeed briefly introduced in the 1950s. The Bank of Canada used moral suasion during 1956-7 to attempt to discourage rationing of small business loans, because of their more limited access to alternative forms of debt than large businesses. But the Bank of Canada (1958) concluded that the attempt had been unsuccessful. It was beyond their remit to direct banks in their allocation of credit, which might have been more effective than moral suasion. The Bank has since consistently resisted requests from the Atlantic provinces particularly[14] for renewed attempts at employing moral suasion. But the Economic Council of Canada (1977) regard use of moral suasion as providing some scope for regionally differentiated monetary policy.

The banks themselves, through the Canadian Bankers' Association (1980), have responded to the suggestion that they favour loans to large corporations over small business loans by emphasising their concern for small business. The Association distributes, in support, a study by Wynant *et al.* (1982), which concludes (page 10) 'that the banks treat small businesses as equitably as they do larger businesses'. Higher loan charges are justified by higher risk and administrative costs, although policy changes of a managerial and organisational nature are advocated to reduce the rejection of viable small business loan applicants. But Dean (1976, 1977) argues that the data show a secular trend of a falling proportion of small business loans which cannot be explained by inflation (raising the value of loan requirements) or changes in the size composition of the business sector. In the early 1970s the banks did attempt to redress the balance by maintaining a dual prime rate, with a lower rate for small business, farmers and fishermen, but since few such borrowers qualified as 'prime' borrowers the program had very limited effect and proved to be unsustainable.[15]

The proposal for regionally differentiated interest rates has been widely rejected on the grounds that arbitrage within the national market would direct the low interest funds into high-interest financial assets, thus eventually eliminating the interest rate differential.[16] Indeed the Macdonald Commission (Government of Canada 1985, p.161) rejects the possibility of regional monetary policy on these grounds alone. Exceptions may however be made in the case of regionally segmented markets, particularly the housing finance market, a possibility suggested by the Economic Council of Canada (1977). Indeed the combination of high market interest rates and a weak housing market in 1982 encouraged the federal government and all four Western provinces to introduce a home mortgage subsidy program. It is possible to argue further that the credit market is regionally segmented for small business, particularly in Peripheral areas. High loan charges for such borrowers are conventionally defined as reflecting high risk; in fact they could reflect local monopoly power among lenders. The appropriate policy response in this case might however be to change the structure of the financial sector rather than by imposing lower interest rates on a regional basis.

A third possibility is to equalise regional interest rates which are currently differentiated in such a way as to disadvantage Peripheral regions. It was demonstrated in chapter four that such differentiation applies to provincial bond issues. A possible solution would be for the Bank of Canada to support provincial bond issues. Courchene (1986, chapter 4) rejects this proposal on the grounds that it would undermine national monetary policy as administered through open market operations. While provincial input into national monetary policy would diminish such a problem, and indeed could be desirable on its own merits, Courchene dismisses the possibility without rationale.

The third possible area of regional monetary policy is banks' reserve requirements. Where there is some regional segmentation of the banking system, as in the UK, it has been possible in the past to impose lower reserve requirements on banks in high unemployment regions (Scotland and Northern Ireland), so that any period of monetary tightness would require a lesser multiple contraction of credit in these regions. (See Gaskin, 1965.) Within a nationwide banking system as in Canada the presence of each bank is still stronger in some regions than others, so regional reserve requirements would arbitrarily alter the relative competitiveness of the banks. More significantly, they would be subject to easy evasion since the location of deposits need bear no relation to the location of the depositor; deposits normally booked in Toronto could be booked in Halifax instead if that would involve a lower reserve cost. Further, since the banks would presumably alter their branch management procedure to break the present connection between branch assets and liabilities, no increase in credit in the low reserve requirement regions could be presumed to follow.

Of the available options[17] for implementing regional monetary policy, moral suasion discouraging rationing of small business loans seems the most promising, although the power to issue directives on credit allocation would greatly increase the policy's effectiveness. The main counter-argument appears to be that persuading banks to behave other than as they would prefer must reduce their profits.[18] For an individual bank, this argument may be sound, although it does not in itself preclude the use of moral suasion (or directives). For the entire banking system the argument is more debatable. If greater credit availability in low-income regions encouraged the growth of small businesses into large businesses, with all the attendant linkage effects including lower liquidity preference among residents, then the banks' long run interests as well as those of the region would indeed be served. In encouraging such a reallocation of credit the Bank of Canada would simply be overcoming the 'prisoners' dilemma'. It is not surprising that, if the monetary authority expresses moral suasion explicitly as being against the banks' own interests, the banks themselves would feel justified in resisting the suasion.

5.4 THE STRUCTURE OF THE FINANCIAL SYSTEM

On the basis of the British North America Act, the federal government has jurisdiction over banking in Canada. Restrictions can therefore be imposed on the structure of bank assets and liabilities. These restrictions have, historically, performed three functions. First, by specifying Bank of Canada liabilities as bank reserves and imposing minimum ratios of reserves to deposits, the federal government has a lever for controlling the total of bank deposits. Second, these ratios and the specification of non-admissible assets (such as certain types of mortgage asset) can be employed for prudential control (as opposed to monetary control). The successful functioning of a banking system depends on confidence in its liabilities. If one bank were unable to honour its liabilities due to an imprudent selection of assets, the resulting erosion of confidence among deposit holders could affect the entire banking system. Third, the federal government can allow either specialisation or competition among financial institutions by specifying the types of asset and liability each class of institution may hold. Since many non-bank financial intermediaries come under provincial jurisdiction, the provincial governments also use their power to influence asset and liability structure to promote prudence as well as specialisation or competition.

The federal and provincial governments can further influence the structure of the financial system by setting up their own financial intermediaries. Beginning with the provincial savings banks in the 1930s, the public sector has attempted to fill perceived gaps in the financial intermediation process. At the present time, the federal government is a major participant in the provision of mortgage finance, export credit, farm credit, and, to a much lesser degree (relative to private sector financing) business credit. (See Economic Council of Canada, 1982b.) In terms of savings instruments, the federal government acquires funds through Treasury bill and bond issues, while two provincial governments (Alberta and Ontario) still run savings institutions, as well as issuing bonds. In general, however, the fund-raising and credit allocation functions are conducted quite separately, without the constraints imposed by market forces on private sector institutions to maintain some balance between asset and liability structure.

The financial structure has come under scrutiny by the Royal Commissions on Banking and Currency (1933) and on Banking and Finance (1964), during the periodic revisions of the Bank Act and by the MacLaren Committee (Government of Canada 1984) and subsequently by Finance Canada (1985). We have seen that this structure (as compared to the US financial structure, for example) has a strong influence on the possibility of regional monetary policy, or the lack of it. In this section we consider more generally the implications of the structure of the financial system for the regional allocation of credit, and various proposals for changing that structure.

The key financial institutions are the banks, in that they have the greatest capacity to create credit. The banks determine the initial regional distribution of money which, by financing activity and generating incomes, is the basis for each region's finance. The redeposit ratio is high for the banking system as a whole, since non-bank financial intermediaries hold bank deposits as reserves; any switch by the public from bank deposits to non-bank deposits is unlikely to alter significantly the volume of bank deposits since most return as non-bank reserves. Even for any one bank the redeposit ratio is high since there are only nine in total. Recent federal proposals (see Government of Canada, 1984 and Finance Canada, 1985) are for breaking down the distinctions between the four pillars of the financial system (the banks, securities dealers, trust companies and insurance companies). The outcome would be to extend the credit creation capacity of the financial system as a whole.

Yet, when the structure of the financial system is under review, it is always in terms of financial intermediation, reallocating existing savings to finance investment. As a result, efficiency in providing appropriate instruments for savers and investors is regarded as the criterion by which the structure should be judged. (For example, homogenisation of the financial system would involve centralised regulation, limiting the capacity of provincial governments to 'misallocate' financial reserves. (See Schultz and Alexandroff, 1986 and Whalley, 1983.) The (Porter) Royal Commission on Banking and Finance (1964, p.8) stated that 'an efficient financial system ... must encourage the transfer of funds from surplus to deficit units'. The Government of Canada (1976, p.8) White Paper preceding the 1980 revisions of the Bank Act stated in similar vein:

> The economic purpose of the financial system is to contribute to the nation's productivity that arises from specialisation and trade by providing the fundamental system for making payments and the basic means whereby savers may accumulate their savings and put them at the disposal of those who require funds to finance consumption, production or capital investments.

In these documents and elsewhere (see Hood, 1958 and Economic Council of Canada, 1976), the conclusion is drawn that the financial system will perform this intermediation function more efficiently the greater the degree of competition. Indeed, in its submission to the Western Economic Opportunities Conference, the federal government identified the interests of the Western region with the capacity of the financial system to channel funds from savers to investors as follows:

> ...the function of the financial system ... is to facilitate the movement of funds between savers and lenders [sic] both within and between areas. Competition between institutions of the same kind and between different kinds of institutions helps to insure [sic] the effective working of the system in carrying out this intermediary rôle. (Government of Canada 1973, p.330.)

Now, if in fact banks generate savings by financing expenditure, rather than lending out existing savings, profit-seeking behaviour becomes self fulfilling (as long as defaults are avoided), and thus cannot be analysed on the basis of static efficiency criteria. Further, profit maximisation justifies the banks in channelling the credit and money creation process away from declining regions. The more efficient the banking system, the more easily capital may be induced to flow out of such regions.

The existing banking structure is not competitive in any normal sense of the term. In 1980, the 'Big Five' banks held 91% of the assets of the eleven chartered banks. Indeed the (Bryce) Royal Commission on Corporate Concentration (1978) noted this high degree of concentration and argued for more competition.

Both the 1967 and 1980 revisions of the Bank Act were put forward as measures to increase competition, but neither seems to have reduced the relative power of the banks. Both sets of revisions included measures to reduce differences between banks and non-bank financial intermediaries. In 1967, the banks were given access to the conventional mortgage market, the six per cent ceiling on loan rates was removed and prohibitions put on interest rate collusion,[19] and reserve requirements were, effectively, reduced. (See Economic Council of Canada 1976.) In 1980, the banks were given access through their subsidiaries to additional classes of asset, such as leasing and factoring, non-bank financial intermediaries were given direct access to the new Canadian Payments Association, and subsidiaries of foreign banks were brought under the net of federal regulation as Schedule B banks, with certain attendant privileges. (See Labrosse, 1980.) From 1967, mergers between banks had to be approved by the Minister of Finance. From 1980, banks could be incorporated by letters patent rather than going through the chartering procedure. Also, provincial governments were now permitted to hold voting equity in new banks, up to twenty-five per cent, to be reduced to a maximum of ten per cent after ten years.

Increased competition in banking did not ensue, primarily because of the unbalanced structure of the banking system. In spite of a rapid rate of growth of the banking system as a whole, the Big Five's share only fell from ninety-three per cent to ninety-one per cent of bank assets between 1967 and 1980. At the same time, the banks' share of the mortgage and consumer loan markets increased significantly. (See Dean and Schwindt, 1976.) By removing scope for segmentation between banks and non-bank financial

141

intermediaries, the measures allowed the already dominant chartered banks to exert market power over a wider field. Certainly the foreign banks pose a competitive threat to the Canadian banks, but the 1980 Bank Act revision brought that threat within a regulatory framework, which explicitly limited their growth. In fact, as a spokesman for one of the major banks has pointed out (see Peters 1976), the only way to increase competition significantly within an industry already so heavily concentrated is to break up the large banks into smaller institutions.

The latest proposals for the financial system (see Government of Canada, 1984, Finance Canada, 1985 and also Royal Commission on the Economic Union and Development Prospects for Canada, 1985) would be likely, similarly, to lead eventually to increased concentration in the financial sector. At the same time, the Canada-US Free Trade Agreement (Government of Canada 1987, article 1703) would open the Canadian financial system up to increased competition from the US: US firms and investors would not be treated as 'foreigners' with respect to the limitations on ownership of Canadian banks, and US bank subsidiaries in Canada would be (individually and collectively) exempt from the sixteen per cent ceiling on the proportion of the Bank sector which may be foreign. Banking history again would suggest that, while the increased competition might initially lead to fragmentation of the banking sector, the ultimate outcome would be increased concentration on a North American scale.

The banking industry cannot, however, be treated like any other industry and concentration can be said to confer social benefits. Banks' product (loans, deposits and payments services) derive their value from the confidence placed in individual banks and the banking system as a whole. Perfect competition in the theoretical sense would require a very large number of small banks, each earning only normal profits and each liable to bankruptcy if costs rise above the industry average. In such an industry, confidence in the liabilities of any one institution would be low and the capacity to finance economic activity would be limited. The US experience here is instructive, however, in showing that a large number of banks on a scale much smaller than Canadian banks can perform effectively, particularly with a deposit insurance scheme. Thus, while some barriers to entry into banking are justified by the social benefits conferred by a stable banking system, this consideration does not provide justification for a banking system as concentrated as it is in Canada.

The second major argument in favour of concentration in banking is the opportunity to reap economics of scale. Jones and Laudadio (1972) have attempted to identify economies of scale for Canadian banks over the period 1955-69. While increasing scale over time appeared to indicate increasing returns from increased inputs, it can be explained by rising labour and capital productivity due to technological advance and 'learning and doing'.[20] Jones and Laudadio show that there is no evidence of economies of scale if, alternatively, cross-section data are used. Their conclusion is confirmed by the (Bryce) Royal Commission on Corporate Concentration (1978, chapter 10).

More work has been done on the economies of scale question in the US, partly because there is a larger statistical sample available, but partly also because there has been a longstanding issue as to whether more bank branching (and thus larger individual banking organisations) might be justified. Estimates differ markedly as to the optimal scale of banks depending on the years studied, the definition of inputs and output, etc. For example, a study of the US by Greenbaum, published in 1966, concludes that most significant economies of scale are reaped by the time assets reach US $10 million. Roughly speaking, in 1966, Canada's total bank assets could have supported 2,750 banks of this size. Guttentag's (1976) optimal bank size (US $15 million deposits) would have suggested arund 7,500 banks in Canada in 1976. The Royal Bank was by this criterion, roughly 1,750 times its optimal size; when the Bank of British Columbia, the smallest in that year, was around 50 times Guttentag's optimal size. Dean and Schwindt's (1976) application of another study to Canadian data suggested that 1,437 banks could have been supported at optimal scale in 1978. While the estimation of cost curves for banks is a hazardous business, as the variance among estimates indicates, the conclusion for Canada is abundantly clear, that all nine chartered banks, but particularly the Big Five are well beyond the stage of reaping economies of scale.

The issue of whether or not banking should be more concentrated must frequently be addressed by policy makers in the US. Where branching is prohibited, concentration occurs through holding company acquisitions or mergers. There is in addition pressure from domestic banks for relaxation of state branching laws and the McFadden Act of 1927 (which limits each federally incorporated bank to only one state's branching laws); foreign banks, not being state or federally incorporated, are subject to no branching limitations. There is thus a wealth of literature on the relative merits of more scope for branching.[21]

Benefits of branching other than economies of scale are cited, such as a broader range of banking services and the breaking up of one-bank-town monopolies. But, as the size of Canadian banks relative to the US optimum indicates, the increase in scale under consideration is still well below that of the Canadian banks. Starting from the present degree of concentration in Canada, it is hard to see the range of services being reduced or the degree of local monopoly increased by more entrants into banking. In any case there is not even unanimity in the US literature that any significant increase in range of services would emerge from more concentration. Yet the federal White Paper prior to the 1980 Bank Act revisions argued for no restrictions on bank size on the grounds that a national branching system is necessary for the wide dispersal of a standard range of services.

It can be argued that a branching system is bound to be more concentrated than a unit banking system, and that comparing the two is illegitimate. On this basis, Short (1979) compared branch banking in Canada instead with Western European countries and Japan, and found that concentration tended to be a negative function of market size. Indeed the federal government partially justifies the concentration in the Canadian system on the grounds that it is necessary for successful competition with foreign banks. But these observations are simply consistent with the notion that, without US-style regulation, banking systems have a natural tendency towards concentration.

Short does note a positive relationship between degree of concentration and profit rates. There is some debate about the pressure of monopoly profits among Canadian banks. The Bryce Commission remained agnostic on the subject of the source of excess profits, although Mintz (1979) later confirmed in detail that, since 1967 at least, Canadian banks had indeed earned excess profits when compared with non-bank financial intermediaries, US banks, and the Canadian manufacturing sector.[22] While the banks explain these high after-tax profits as resulting from increased risk, increased efficiency and increased foreign business, the Economic Council of Canada (1976) explained it by an increase in market power following the 1967 Bank Act revision, an increase made possible according to Mintz by strong barriers to entry into banking. In 1982, both the BC and Manitoba governments singled out the higher profits of banks by imposing on them a special tax under the corporation capital tax system. (See Government of Manitoba, 1982.)

The question of particular interest here is how this concentration affects loan charges and the regional allocation of credit. The combination of relatively high profit rates and operation at a scale well above that at which average cost is at a minimum certainly imply some element of monopoly pricing. Indeed the Economic Council of Canada (1976) explicitly advocated increased competition as a means of reducing yield spreads. Since posted interest rates do vary by region in the US, it is possible to reach some conclusions about the relationship between interest rates on loans and degree of concentration. Meyer (1967) and Phillips (1967) found loan rates higher the greater the degree of banking concentration, although others (Flechsig, 1965, and Taylor, 1968) argue that rate differences are explained more by loan size and location of bank. On the latter point, they identify rates as being higher in regions where demand for money is strong relative to supply, as we have done here for Canada.

In terms of the influence of concentration on asset portfolios, the US evidence is again difficult to interpret because of the multiplicity of factors involved in each bank's behavior. Most studies conclude that the ratio of loans to deposits is higher for branch banks or unit banks owned by holding companies, than for solitary unit banks.[23]   This evidence is based on 'micro' data, observing the change in behavior of a unit bank when taken over by a holding company, for example. The lower loan/deposit ratio of unit banks is explained by the greater need for liquidity in the absence of a parent company to make up any shortfall of funds. But the change to higher loan/deposit ratios on takeover could be explained by the fact that it is banks which are not fulfilling their full profit potential which are most likely to be taken over.

The macro evidence, looking at aggregate lending behavior by size of bank and by region suggests some tendency for loan/deposit ratios to be higher among larger banks and regions of higher degrees of banking concentration. The loans to total assets ratio is however clearly higher in low bank concentration areas and those remote from financial centres, because of much lower recourse to the federal funds market relative to deposits (in spite of higher holdings of federal funds assests). However, a higher loan/deposit or loan/asset ratio does not imply anything about the proportion of local deposits relative to local loans, since the loans could be extended to a borrower in any other region. Nevertheless, the higher the degree of concentration, the lower the proportion of assets consisting of loans for agriculture, commerce and industry. Further, securities held by these smaller, local banks tend to include a higher proportion of local securities. (See Dow, 1981, chapter nine.)

Since the loan/deposit ratio has been used in the US literature as an indicator of how far banks 'syphon off' local savings for lending elsewhere it is interesting to look at the Canadian banks' loan/deposit ratios. These are shown for 1960, 1970, 1976 and 1980 in Table 5.1 for the 'Big Five' banks together and the other six banks. The 'other' six banks are significantly smaller in size, and also with business more concentrated in particular regions, than the Big Five. The ratio is consistently higher for the 'other banks'. After the 1967 lifting of the six per cent loan rate ceiling, it was to be expected that the ratio would rise, but the relatively poor state of the economy in 1970 would be expected to increase liquidity preference on the part of the banks sufficiently to offset that trend. As a matter of interest, these can be compared with the ratios for the large US banks, shown in Table 5.2 for 1978. The 'Big Five' ratio is similar to that for the New York City banks, and the 'others' to their counterparts in the US. Chicago stands out as an interesting exception, with a particularly high loan/deposit ratio. There is no branching at all in Chicago.

The Canadian government's position against promoting a less concentrated banking system reflects views expressed in the US about the inefficiency of the unit banking system. The sources of inefficiency can be categorised as follows:

1)   bank portfolios being kept more liquid, for prudential reasons, than would be necessary in a more concentrated system,

2)   the free movement of funds being impeded by institutional rigidities within a fragmented banking system,

3)   the practical difficulties involved in cheque transactions between a multitude of banks.

Table 5.1
Loan/Deposit Ratio (%) by Size of Bank*

	1966	1970	1976	1980
'Big Five' Banks	64.6	60.0	68.1	69.1
Other Banks	65.8	65.0	75.1	74.2

* 'Big Five':   Royal Bank, Canadian Imperial Bank of Commerce, Bank of Montreal, Bank of Nova Scotia and Toronto-Dominion Bank.

Other: National Bank (Banque Canadienne Nationale and Banque Provincial for 1966-76), Mercantile Bank (now merged with the National Bank), Bank of British Columbia, Continental Bank, Northland Bank and Canadian Commercial Bank (both 1975-1985). The Bank of Alberta and the Western and Pacific Bank of Canada were set up after this period, in 1984.

Source: Annual Reports.

Table 5.2
Loan/Deposit Ratio (%) by Class of Bank
United States 1978

Member Banks*

Large	(New York City	69.7
	(City of Chicago	89.5
	(Other	75.0
All Other		67.3

Non-Member Bank* 67.4

*   Membership refers to the Federal Reserve System. Non-members are on average smaller banks than members of the system.

Source: *Federal Reserve Bulletin* September 1980.

147

Certainly the latter source of inefficiency is an important one, but it is not insurmountable. Innovations in European banking, for example, allow cheque cashing in a range of countries when backed up by a cheque card honoured by an international group of banks. Developments towards nationwide funds transfer systems in retail outlets as well as financial institutions would help to overcome the information problems currently involved in dealing with a large number of little known banks.

The other two factors are not so clear-cut as sources of inefficiency particularly when taken in conjunction with the costs of regional policy. If locally-oriented banks extend credit primarily locally, even if the loan/deposit ratio is relatively low, the absolute amount of local credit may be higher than that extended by a branch bank. If, as a result, the local economy is more viable, then the liquidity preference of local businesses, households and other local financial institutions will be lower than would otherwise be the case, allowing higher local deposit levels and thus higher local credit creation. It cannot then be concluded which situation would involve the higher liquid asset ratio for all sectors and thus which was the more efficient.

Again, taking a similar broad view, the efficiency involved in mobile financial resources is not self-evident. Within a static framework, it is efficient to seek the highest returns. But the decision to concentrate credit creation in one region itself alters returns in other regions. Institutional impediments to those capital flows which are either seeking short-term gain regardless of long-term effects, or simply following individual bank interest rather than the collective interest, can be efficient in the long-run, or from a collective point of view, respectively.

Naylor (1975) argues that the eastern seaboard of the US succeeded in avoiding the type of decline, as the frontier moved west, which the Atlantic provinces experienced. He ascribes this success to the existence of a unit banking system which continued to create credit in that region, in contrast to the Canadian system which allowed the free movement of credit creation to other regions. Indeed, the American experience has been one of steadily narrowing per capita regional income differentials; Canada's experience has been less fortunate. The reasons for this difference in experience are highly complex. But it does not seem unreasonable to surmise that a regionally segmented banking system played some part.

The federal government has acknowledged the particular difficulties of small business borrowers in regions remote from the financial centre. (See Government of Canada, 1973.) And indeed both the federal and provincial governments have set up lending agencies to fill perceived gaps in the financial system. Particularly in the business loan market, however, the government presence is very limited. A recent Economic Council of Canada (1982b) report, assessing government intervention in financial markets does so using the criterion of efficiency. The presumption is that credit gaps appear as a result of market imperfections, which government should help to correct. Government financial assistance in the form of subsidised loans is viewed as an undesirable vehicle for pursuing goals other than correcting market imperfections because they distort relative prices and thus impede the free working of market forces.

Quite apart from the (important) question of how effectively such programmes are implemented and coordinated, which the Council's report pursues at some length, it has been suggested here that unfettered market forces are not necessarily efficient, particularly from the viewpoint of regional development. This view is supported by the conclusion of the Roy (1986) report that freedom of capital movements not be enshrined in the constitution but rather be encouraged by a code of conduct, a suggestion taken up by the Royal Commission on the Economic Union and Development Prospects for Canada (1985). A key variable determining regional capital flows is the state of expectations as to the future of a regional economy. Even if a programme is inefficient in terms of the number of people employed, or the financial return, it achieves its aims of promoting regional development if the programme, and the governmental will it represents, bolster expectations in a self-fulfilling way.

These programmes for business finance however are small compared to the volume of bank lending. We now turn to considering proposals for altering the structure of the banking system itself with a view to promoting more balanced regional development. They fall into the following categories:

(i)   provincial government-owned banks.
(ii)   more active provincial promotion of private sector non-bank financial intermediaries.
(iii)   provincial government-sponsored regional financial centres.

The most direct method of influencing the regional allocation of credit and the loan charges imposed, is to have a largely or entirely public sector banking system. Although politically such a solution might be regarded as impractical, economically it is quite practical. Even before the Mitterand government took power in France, nationalising the entire banking system, around sixty per cent of banking was already owned by the public sector. A public sector banking system *could* be run on strict profit-maximising principles (with profits going into general revenues). But where such principles cut across social priorities, public ownership would provide the opportunity for establishing alternative criteria. Serious objections have not been raised by the business community about political influence on the Bank of Canada (although the tight monetary policy which contributed to the recent recession was not apparently in the interests of business). Nor has there been any questioning of the motives behind credit allocation by Alberta Treasury offices. It is not apparent that a public sector banking system should be any more subject to political influence in the sense of promoting politicians' own interests. (See Government of Canada, 1973 and Canadian Bankers' Association, 1974.)

In the absence of such a sweeping solution, the provincial governments themselves could establish banks in their own provinces. Legislation was drafted but never enacted in British Columbia to set up a Savings and Trust Corporation with the powers, if not the name, of a bank. All four Western provinces at the 1973 Western Economic Opportunities Conference asked for the right to hold unlimited equity in banks. As a result, the federal government agreed to allow a maximum twenty-five per cent equity in a new bank, declining to ten per cent in ten years.

The federal government's WEOC position paper, aside from objecting to segmentation of the banking system on the efficiency grounds discussed above, argued that private sector regional interests already had free entry into the banking system. The implication was that the Western provinces were claiming a need which was not in fact there. In fact the evidence suggests quite significant barriers to entry (see Economic Council of Canada, 1976), which raise questions as to the viability of private provincial banks starting up

150

in a well-established oligopolistic industry. The evidence suggests that the Canadian market is overbranched due to the attempts of the chartered banks to maintain market share. (See Dean, 1976.) Theory of oligopolistic markets would predict collusive pricing behaviour and other practices designed to squeeze out an unwanted entrant to the industry.

The primary purpose of a provincial bank would be to meet service and credit needs not provided by the existing banks. In doing so, opening branches in rural areas, making small business loans, etc. there is a risk that the government bank might simply be taking a share of the actual, or potential, non-bank financial intermediary market, particularly credit unions and caisses populaires, rather than institutions like trust companies which operate in an oligopolistic market similar to the banks. Indeed, the Manitoba credit unions and caisses populaires put this argument to the Manitoba government in response to a proposal for Government Treasury branches.[25] They suggested that the government, with its jurisdiction over credit unions, could instead subsidise credit union branches opened in remote areas and extend subsidised credit to particular types of borrowers through the existing credit union structure. By thus promoting the credit union movement, the provincial governments could help to increase competition between the banks and the credit unions.

Proposals have been put forward for Quebec which would strengthen the non-bank financial sector as well as restoring Montreal to its position of financial centre. Advocating freedom of capital movements, particularly between Quebec and other countries, the Quebec report on savings (Government of Quebec, 1980) makes recommendations designed to increase the efficiency and competitiveness of Quebec financial markets. The most effective means of achieving this is seen as government promotion of non-bank financial intermediaries through liberalising regulation rather than promoting entry into the banking system. The report identifies the problem as being relatively high savings in Quebec not been translated into availability of funds in an appropriate form to finance economic development. The encouragement of a broader range of borrowing and lending instruments provided by Quebec institutions would allow improved financial intermediation. Direct government involvement in the allocation of credit is seen as violating, as well as being rendered impossible by, the desired degree of capital mobility.

Ryba (1974a) goes further in rejecting direct government involvement in financial markets in terms of influencing the flow of funds. He argues rather in favour of government establishment of a financial centre which would promote the growth of Quebec markets in stocks, bonds and money by providing research and other service facilities. This is not put forward as a general solution for all Canadian regions, because, he suggests, Quebec has a more developed secondary sector than the Atlantic and Prairie regions, and has a history of financial eminence to draw on. Both sets of recommendations for Quebec start from the position that Quebec's financial problems stem from market imperfections.

While both sets of Quebec proposals, for promotion of non-bank financial intermediaries and of a financial centre, would be constructive in challenging the market power of the chartered banks, particularly those based in Toronto, their effect would be limited. In both cases, the theoretical basis is the orthodox one which is founded on faith in market forces. Liberalising non-bank financial intermediaries' legislation is a start, but it is unreasonable to expect them to compete successfully with the chartered banks without much more positive intervention on the part of the provincial government. Similarly, liberalising capital flows, particularly with other countries, is just as likely to lead to outflows as to inflows unless the development of the financial centre is combined with some restrictions on capital flows. The proposals represent only the first step of a successful strategy.

The steps taken following these proposals in fact actively discourage capital outflows. They use the provincial tax system to encourage capital retention in Quebec and promote the Quebec financial sector. According to the Quebec Stock Savings Plan set up in 1979, tax incentives are made available for the purchase of stocks in approved Quebec companies (subject to various restrictions, such as a minimum period for holding the stock and maximum tax credits for any one taxpayer). Similar schemes have been introduced in Alberta and Saskatchewan, and are under consideration in Nova Scotia and British Columbia. In addition, the Quebec government has introduced a Quebec deposit insurance scheme for its financial institutions, in an effort to increase confidence in the provincial financial sector. Further, the tax system has been used to encourage the formation of new financial institutions in Quebec.

These measures have promoted some concern that they may lead to an inefficient misallocation of resources. (See, e.g. Whalley, 1983.) Indeed the MacLaren Committee (Government of Canada, 1984) advocates a change in regulatory regime which would in effect bring non-bank financial intermediation and securities trading more under centralised, federal control. The Macdonald Commission Report (Royal Commission on the Economic Union and Development Prospects for Canada, 1985) also was concerned about the effect on resource allocation and advocated increased capital mobility within Canada; the Commission did however consider that the amounts involved in provincial schemes were too small to cause any significant crowding out. Nevertheless, Courchene (1986) argued against increased federal jurisdiction over the financial sector because it would increase scope for impediments to international capital flows, which he considered to be a potentially more serious source of resource misallocation.

Nevertheless, as Schultz and Alexandroff (1986, p.125) point out:

> If the federal and provincial governments insist on directing further industrial change, then far greater attention must be paid to altering the financial system in this country to enable state direction to proceed with some chance of success

As Whalley (1983) puts it from a static general equilibrium perspective, there may be a second best argument for exercise of provincial jurisdiction to 'distort' capital flows. But from a dependency theory perspective, the question is more one of the dynamics of development. Market forces encourage concentration in the financial sector and dependence of Peripheral regions on inflows of outside capital. Provincial jurisdiction over securities trading and non-bank financial intermediaries provides some leverage to counter the effect of market forces. But, as the financial sector proceeds to concentrate nationally and internationally, the reach of provincial jurisdiction (particularly in the Peripheral provinces) will become progressively more limited. Federal support of regional goals needs to be translated into active federal involvement in encouraging credit creation in Peripheral regions and discouraging capital outflows which have no rationale in production conditions, no matter what the division of regulatory powers.

5.5 CONCLUSION

The first question to face up to in discussing regional policy relates to the strength of political commitment to reducing regional disparities. Such a political question in some sense is ancillary to the study of how best to reduce disparities when the political will to do so exists. At one level it does determine, however, how regional policy is put across. In the international sphere redistribution in favour of developing countries is often presented as an efficient means of increasing effective demand for developed country products. So regionally differentiated fiscal and monetary policy is often presented as the efficient solution to pursuing national goals within a regionally diverse country. The implication is that it is to general advantage for regional disparities to be reduced.

At another level, however, the political economy of regional policy is inextricably tied up with the explanation for the persistence of regional disparities in the first place. Political power is not independent of the power of accumulation, the driving force of the economy. Successful accumulation is served by upward valuations of assets and low costs, and thus by speculative financial markets on the one hand and concentration in economic activity on the other. The market forces which have exacerbated initial tendencies towards regional disparity are not obviously benefited by attempts to reduce those disparities.

The explanation for disparities governs not only the political feasibility of reducing them, but also the particular policy tools chosen. Matthews (1981, 1983) contrasts dependency theory, as it is used here, with what Courchene calls 'transfer dependency theory'. Courchene sees regional policy in the form of transfer payments, combined with impediments to labour markets like minimum wage legislation, as preventing the disappearance of disparities. Matthews rather sees the capital outflows occurring within relatively free financial markets as being a major contributory factor in maintaining

154

disparities. If market forces are identified as the problem, then some modification of market forces must be the solution.

While financial factors have been stressed here, regional policy should be addressed to the underlying real disparities in resource endowment, labour productivity, etc., as much as to financial matters. But the two cannot really be separated neatly into compartments. It is financial markets as much as anything else which determine the value of output and thus return on investment. To the extent that lack of liquidity has led to concentration of ownership in industry as well as foregone expenditure plans, money and finance have played a significant part in perpetuating disparities. As a corollary, regional polilcy which brings with it new money, and a burst of confidence in the liquidity of local assets will ease the recipient region's actual illiquidity, promote new investment plans and the funds to finance it through financial institutions.

Given the existing financial structure, most observers are probably correct in their conclusions about the feasibility of regional monetary policy in general. The case for moral suasion is however 'not proven'. If the Bank of Canada attempts to encourage more lending in declining regions during periods of monetary squeeze, as a sacrificial contribution by the banking system it is not likely to be a success. But if at the same time the government is itself actually promoting activity in these regions, then the risk to the banks would be diminished. Indeed, as the Economic Council of Canada (1982b) advocates, government guarantees on bank loans, rather than government loans, may be the most effective way of reducing rationing in declining regions.

But even if such lending were not to the banks' best advantage, it is not clear that that in itself constitutes a sufficient counter-argument. Bank profits are by most reckonings excessive, the result at least in part of the barriers to entry which are deemed necessary for the stability of the industry. It does not seem unreasonable for the banks to accept moral suasion (or directives if need be) to modify their own portfolio particularly when monetary policy is tight, as responsible national corporate citizens.

More direct means of altering the allocation of credit would involve government-owned banks. Further, the public sector could promote more competition in the financial sector, as well as more regional segmentation, by promoting local non-bank financial intermediaries, particularly credit unions and caisses populaires. In the US, the thrift institutions have been given entry into the commercial loan business, posing a competitive threat to the banks, while a similar development has been advocated for Britain's building societies. (See *The Economist*, April 9, 1983, p,8.) Credit unions and caisses populaires of course already make commercial loans, but their presence in the market could be bolstered by provisions for provincial government deposits, government loan guarantees and subsidies, and more flexible regulation (avoiding long-standing interest rate ceilings, for example). Such increased provincial government involvement would require great care, given the democratic basis of these institutions. But it is something that they might welcome, if broached in a cooperative spirit, in their competition with the big banks.[26]

Historically, increased government involvement is an appropriate solution for Canada. As Phillips (1978) concludes from his study of Canada's regional disparities, the public sector has been the primary source of entrepreneurship in the past and can be expected to be so in the future, given the opportunity. Financial institutions in contrast have generally been regarded as an independent force, to be given its head. Government savings banks, Heritage Funds in Alberta and Saskatchewan, and the various government lending agencies have played an important part in the redistribution of existing funds. In the monetary area, the allocation of new credit, the banks unquestionably dominate. But the federal government has jurisdiction over the banks, and thus the scope for influencing the way in which new money is allocated, as a tool of regional policy.

Footnotes

[1]   Boadway and Flatters (1981) show that, with conditions including wages fixed above marginal product in low productivity regions, positive migration costs, and an absence of constant returns to scale in the high productivity regions, national efficiency would be increased by employment-promotion by government in the low-productivity regions as an alternative to migration.

[2]   In Marxist language, the capitalist process requires the existence of a reserve army of unemployed. Mandel (1973) uses this concept to explain the persistence of relatively high unemployment in particular regions.

[3]   The formula by which equalisation payments are calculated is a complex one; see Economic Council of Canada (1982a) for a full description. The major exception to the general description given here is that non-oil and gas producing provinces are not fully compensated for not having access to oil and gas revenues. The formula has distorted provincial taxation and revenue policy in order to maximise equalisation payments. For example, a side-effect of channelling resource revenues into a Heritage Fund is that general revenues seem smaller.

[4]   The supermultiplier concept was introduced into regional income mutliplier analysis by Wilson (1968).

[5]   See Dow (1982) for a full elaboration of this point, and Section three below.

[6]   See Auld (1978), Barber (1966), Economic Council of Canada (1982a), Fortin (1982), Maxwell and Pestieau (1980) and Wilson (1977).

[7]   For a discussion of the regional transmission of monetary policy in the US, see Hogan and Kaufman (1977), Miller (1978), Ruffin (1968), Scott (1955), Straszheim (1971) and Thurston (1976).

[8]   See Economic Council of Canada (1968, Chapter 7) and Blain, Patterson and Rae (1974).

[9]   Premiers of Manitoba, Alberta, Saskatchewan and British Columbia (1973).

[10]   The significance of financial constraints on Maritime industry has been a matter of some debate. See chapters three and four.

[11]   There has been considerable work done in the US on the effects of financial innovation on the demand for money, particularly dating from Goldfeld's (1976) study which attempted to explain periodic downward shifts in the US demand for money function.

[12]   This type of question is addressed, using bank (or money) multiplier analysis in Miller (1978) and Moore and Hill (1982).

[13]   The (Bryce) Royal Commission on Corporate Concentration (1978) noted this paradoxical phenomenon.

[14]   See Lounsbury (1960) and Passaris (1975, 1976, 1977). Cairncross (1961) also makes the case for the use of moral suasion.

[15]   See Binhammer and Williams (1976) and Premiers of Manitoba, Alberta, Saskatchewan and British Columbia (1973).

[16]   This argument is put forward by the Government of Canada (1973), the Economic Council of Canada (1968, 1977), Cairncross (1961) and Gaskin (1960), among others.

[17]   An additional vehicle for promoting independent regional monetary policy would be separate regional currencies. But even the Parti Quebecois rejected this policy proposal on taking power (see Government of Quebec 1979) on the grounds that separate currencies within Canada were impractical.

[18]   See Government of Canada (1973) Royal Commission on Banking and Finance (1964, pp.476-7) and Rickover (1976).

[19]   The spirit of the prohibition was broken by an arrangement in 1969 between the banks and the Bank of Canada to limit interest rate competition, and the 1972 Winnipeg Agreement among the banks on deposit rate ceilings.

[20]   This explanation is confirmed by Benston's (1972) study of economies of scale in US banking.

[21]   The literature is surveyed by Guttentag (1976), Fischer and Davis (1976) and McCall (1980).

[22]   See also Economic Council of Canada (1976), Dean (1976, 1977), Sultan (1977) and Peters (1976).

[23]   See Guttentag (1976), Fischer and Davis (1976) and McCall (1980).

[24]   See Mingo (1975) and Curry (1978), although Curry (1981) later revised his opinion that taken-over banks are atypical.

[25]   Co-operative Credit Society of Manitoba and La Centrale des Caisses Populaires du Manitoba (1974).

[26]   This increased government involvement was in fact suggested by the Manitoba credit unions as an alternative to the contemplated Treasury branches. See footnote 25.

6 Conclusion

Economic development is a complex process. It is a process determined not only by physical factor endowments, but by the institutional environment (not least in the form of the state), and by the interdependence between economies. The significance of interdependence is most apparent in the context of regional economic development. The interdependence takes the form not only of trading patterns, but also of financial behaviour.

What has emerged from the foregoing study of the Canadian experience of financial behaviour, as it has affected regional development, is that the financial behavior of all sectors is relevant, not just that of the banks. It is understandable, nevertheless, that the focus of attention should have been on the banks, given Canada's historical experience. In the early years of regional settlement the financial system acted primarily as intermediaries, redistributing saving to finance investment, and allocating new credit to finance investment in different regions, subject to a national reserves constraint. Bankers' judgement as to which projects should be financed, given that constraint, was thus crucial. That judgement was inevitably influenced by the institutional structure of the banking system, which has always been concentrated.

Other sectors were not always passive in the face of what they regarded as unwarranted rationing of credit on the part of the banks. Attempts to establish private banks as alternative sources of credit succeeded in some cases. But the regulatory environment was always conducive to concentration, so that private banks could not aspire to the scale of the large national banks. As development generated wealth, therefore, it was the banks which attracted the financial resources in a cumulative, self-fulfilling process of increasing confidence in bank assets. The credit union movement also represents an attempt to develop alternative sources of credit and repositories for savings. But again, in circular fashion, their scale has limited their ability to inspire the same confidence as the banks, thus limiting their capacity to increase in size.

Although the banks are not constrained by a fixed stock of reserves in the same way that they once were, the supply of credit is by no means limitless. The highly centralised nature of the banking system is bound to lead to a different regional pattern of credit creation than would a decentralised system. This is reinforced by behaviour in the face of increasing liquidity preference in regions where decline is anticipated; the outflow of funds to central financial institutions, depressing local asset values, simply reinforces expectations of decline and the unwillingness of financial institutions to extend credit.

Much of Canada's particular experience of uneven regional development, therefore, can be attributed to the centralised financial system with the implications for the regional pattern of credit creation and the means by which attempts are made by the non-bank sector to satisfy liquidity preference. (The two are interdependent.)

In a sense, the outcome is inevitable within capitalist economies. The underlying motive of financial accumulation on the part of all sectors ensures an outcome whereby finance is allocated in such a way as to attract highest expected financial returns. This in turn encourages financial concentration. Industrial concentration is the general outcome of recessionary conditions as a means of protecting the rate of profit, but financial concentration occurs also to maintain confidence in the product: money.

But such an interpretation is too simplistic. The regulatory environment need not have been so favourable to concentration. The United States provides the obvious counterexample, where decentralisation of financial institutions, and a regional segmentation of financial markets was the result of deliberate policy. Market forces have increasingly broken down this decentralisation and segmentation. But the fact remains, that through the formative years of the States' economic development, the financial system was more attuned to the needs of all regions than was the case in Canada.

The financial system in Canada, as in the United States, is currently in a state of flux. The dominance of the large national banks is being threatened by the encroachment of the trust companies into banking functions, and by the opening up of the banking system to foreign banks. As far as the trust companies are concerned, banking history tells us that market forces will lead to concentration within the larger pool of banks and trust companies; the trust company sector is already dominated by the large trusts in Toronto. In time-honoured fashion the opening up of new banks in the west as a result of the oil boom could not maintain its impetus in the face of the oil slump; the effective financial centre had always remained in Toronto. Recent discussion of promoting the establishment of international financial centres in Vancouver and Montreal, however, pointed the way to one marginal possibility for inhibiting centralising market forces; but the countervailing power of financial interests in Toronto ensured that the federal proposals foundered.

The entry of foreign banks into the Canadian banking sector (although not yet on a regulatory par with domestic banks) raises further issues. Must Canadian banks be concentrated in order to compete on a world scale? Studies on the optimal scale of banks indicate that Canadian banks are so much larger than any reasonable estimate of an optimum that the scale argument cannot be sustained. (Even if it were sustained, there is still scope for government regulation of the regional distribution of credit, although such an approach is very difficult operationally.)

But in fact, the fear of foreign competition in banking has its source in the same factors which cause poorer regions to be disadvantaged by a concentrated national financial system. Underlying the fear is the expectation that the control of the creation and distribution of credit would go out of the hands of the domestic banks, and that the outcome would be a different distribution. In particular, if Canada were to fare badly relative to other economies, credit creation would be less than if it were

161

controlled by the domestic banks, further worsening economic conditions and reducing the value of Canadian assets. This process would be reinforced by an increasing tendency for Canadians to redeposit in foreign banks for liquidity preference reasons. International market forces already ensure that these two interdependent factors have been at work in Canada for some time. But the change in the regulatory environment to allow limited entry by foreign banks has encouraged them. If these banks were allowed to branch, then these factors would become progressively more significant.

International market forces are essentially the same as domestic market forces, with only national financial regulation keeping them apart. The widespread understanding of the consequences of international market forces for the Canadian financial system and the Canadian economy contrasts with widely diverging views about the regional equivalent of these forces. But the sooner there is a realisation that the regional argument is equivalent to the national argument, the greater the possibilities for introducing a regulatory framework which would moderate the domestic forces for uneven regional development.

Bibliography

Acheson, T.N. (1972), 'The National Policy and the Industrialization
of the Maritimes, 1880-1920', *Acadiensis*, Vol.1, Spring.

Acheson, T.N. (1977), 'The Maritimes and 'Empire Canada', in
Bercuson, D.J.(ed.), *Canada and the Burden of Unity*, Macmillan, Toronto.

Addison, J.T., Burton, J. and Torrance, T.S. (1980), 'On the Causes
of Inflation', *The Manchester School*, Vol.48, June.

Addison, J.T., Burton, J. and Torrance, T.S. (1984), 'Causation,
Social Science and Sir John Hicks', *Oxford Economic Papers*, N S Vol.36,
March.

Amin, S. (1974), *Accumulation on a World Scale*, Monthly Review
Press, New York.

Archibald, G.C. (1969), 'The Phillips Curve and the Distribution of Unemployment', *American Economic Review*, Vol.59, May.

Asimakopulos, T. (1983), 'Kalecki and Keynes on Finance, Investment and Saving', *Cambridge Journal of Economics*, Vol.7, September/December.

Asimakopulos, T. (1985), 'Finance, Saving and Investment in Keynes's Economics: A Comment', *Cambridge Journal of Economics*, Vol.9, December.

Asimakopulos, T. (1986a), 'Richardson on Asimakopulos on Finance: A Reply', *Cambridge Journal of Economics*, Vol.10, June.

Asimakopulos, T. (1986b), Finance, Liquidity, Saving and Investment. *Journal of Post Keynesian Economics*, Vol.9, Fall.

Auld, D. (1978), 'Decentralizing Fiscal Policy' in Auld, D. *et al., Canadian Confederation at the Crossroads, Fraser Institute, Vancouver.*

Bank of Canada (1958), Annual Report.

Baran, P. (1957), La Economie Politica del Crecimiento, *FCE, Mexico.*

Barber, C.L. (1966), Theory of Fiscal Policy as Applied to a Province, *study prepared for the Ontario Committee on Taxation, reprinted in part in Waterman, A.M.C., Hum, D.P.J., and Scarfe, B.L. (eds.), (1982),* The Collected Economic Papers of C L Barber, *ISER, Winnipeg.*

Barrett, L.G. (1980), 'Perspectives on Dependency and Under-development in the Atlantic Region', Canadian Review of Sociology and Anthropology, *Vol.17, August.*

Benson, J.N. (1978), Provincial Government Banks: A Case Study of Regional Response to National Institutions, *Fraser Institute, Vancouver.*

Benston, G.J. (1972), 'Economies of Scale of Financial Institutions', Journal of Money, Credit and Banking, *Vol.4, May.*

Benton, S.B. (1974), Small Business Finance in the Atlantic Region, *Atlantic Provinces Economic Council, Halifax.*

Binhammer, H.H. and Williams, J. (1976) *Deposit-Taking Institutions: Innovation and the Process of Change*, Economic Council of Canada, Ottawa.

Blain, L., Patterson, D.G., and Rae, J.D. (1974), 'The Regional Impact of Economic Fluctuations during the Inter-War Period: The Case of British Columbia', *Canadian Journal of Economics*, Vol.7, August.

Boadway, R. and Flatters, F. (1981), 'The Efficiency Basis for Regional Employment Policy', *Canadian Journal of Economics*, Vol.14, February.

Boltz, P.W. (1977), 'Survey of Terms of Bank Lending: New Series', *Federal Reserve Bulletin*, Vol.63, May.

Breckenridge, R.M. (1894), *The Canadian Banking System, 1817-1890*, University of Toronto Thesis.

Brown, V. (1918-9), 'The Western Frontier and the Bank', *Journal of the Canadian Bankers' Association*, Vol. 26, April 1919.

Brym, R.J. and Sacouman, R.J. (1979), *Underdevelopment and Social Movements in Atlantic Canada*, New Hogtown Press, Toronto.

Cairncross, A.K. (1961), *Economic Development and the Atlantic Provinces*, Atlantic Provinces Research Board, Fredericton.

Canadian Bankers' Association (1974), 'Governments' Place in Bank Ownership: The Industry View', *CBA Bulletin*, Vol.17, February, special edition.

Canadian Bankers Association (1978), *Factbook: Chartered Banks of Canada, 1977-78*, CBA, Toronto.

Canadian Bankers' Association (1980), 'The Rôle of the Chartered Banks in Small Business Financing', *CBA Bulletin*, Vol.23, February, special edition.

Cardoso, F.H. and Falletto, E. (1969), *Dependencia y desarollo en America Latina: ensayo de interpretacion sociologica*, Siglo Veintiuno, Mexico.

Carroll, W. (1982), 'The Canadian Corporate Elite: Financiers or Finance Capitalists?', *Studies in Political Economy*, Vol.8, Summer.

Chick, V. (1986), 'The Evolution of the Banking System and the Theory of Saving, Investment and Interest', *Economies et Societes*, Vol.20, *Monnaie et Production 3*.

Chick, V. and Dow, S.C. (1988), 'A Post-Keynesian Perspective on the Relation Between Banking and Regional Development, *Thames Papers in Political Economy*, Spring, reprinted in Arestis, P. (ed.), *Post Keynesian Monetary Economics*, Elgar, Aldershot.

Coddington, A. (1975) 'The Rationale of General Equilibrium Theory', *Economic Inquiry*, Vol. 13, December.

Cooley, T.F. and LeRoy, S.F. (1981), 'Identification and Estimation of Money Demand', *American Economic Review*, Vol.71, December.

Cooperative Commonwealth Federation (1933), *Regina Manifesto*.

Cooperative Credit Society of Manitoba and La Centrale Des Caisses Populaires du Manitoba (1974), *Submission to the Government of Manitoba with respect to the matter of Treasury Branches Establishment*, Winnipeg, May.

Courchene, T.J. (1978), 'Avenues of Adjustment: The Transfer System and Regional Disparities', in Auld, D. *et al., Canadian Confederation at the Crossroads*, Fraser Institute, Vancouver.

Courchene, T.J. (1981), 'A Market Perspective on Regional Disparities', *Canadian Public Policy*, Vol.7, Autumn.

Courchene, T.J. (1986), *Economic Management and the Division of Powers*, Research Study No. 67, University of Toronto Press, Toronto, for the Royal Commission on the Economic Union and Development Prospects for Canada.

Curry, T.J. (1978), 'The Performance of Bank Holding Companies', in *The Bank Holding Company Movement to 1978 - A Compendium*, Federal Research Board, Washington, D.C., September.

Curry, T.J. (1981), 'The Pre-Acquisition Characteristics of Banks Acquired by Multibank Holding Companies', *Journal of Bank Research*, Vol.12, Summer.

Davidson, P. (1986), 'Finance, Funding, Saving and Investment', *Journal of Post Keynesian Economics*, Vol.9, Fall.

Dean, J.W. (1976), 'The 1977 Bank Act: Comment', *Canadian Public Policy*, Vol.2, Summer.

Dean, J.W. (1977), 'Papers on the 1977 Bank Act Revision: A Reply', *Canadian Public Policy*, Vol.3, Winter.

Dean, J.W. and Schwindt, R. (1976), 'Bank Act Revision in Canada: Past and Potential Effects on Market Structure and Competition', *Banca Nazionale del Lavoro Quarterly Review*, Vol.116, March.

Donner, A.W. (1982), *Financing the Future: Canada's Capital Markets in the Eighties*, Canadian Institute for Economic Policy, Ottawa.

Douglas, C.H. (1937), *The Alberta Experiment*, Eyre and Spottiswoode, London.

Dow, S.C. (1981), *Money and Real Economic Disparities Between Nations and Between Regions*, University of Glasgow PhD Thesis.

Dow, S.C. (1982), 'The Regional Composition of the Money Multiplier Process', *Scottish Journal of Political Economy*, Vol.29, February.

Dow, S.C. (1985), *Macroeconomic Thought: A Methodological Approach*, Basil Blackwell, Oxford and New York.

Dow, S.C. (1987a) 'Banking and Regional Development in Canada', *British Journal of Canadian Studies*, Vol. 2, June.

Dow, S.C. (1987b) 'Money and Regional Development', *Studies in Political Economy*, Vol. 23, Summer.

Dow, S.C. and Earl, P.E. (1982), *Money Matters: A Keynesian Approach to Monetary Economics*, Martin Robertson, Oxford.

Easterbrook, W.T. and Aitken, H.G.J. (1956), *Canadian Economic History*, Macmillan, Toronto.

Eaton, G.H. and Bond, D.E. (1970), 'Canada's Newest Money Market - Vancouver', *The Canadian Banker*, Vol.77, November-December.

Economic Council of Canada (1968), *Fifth Annual Review: the Challenge of Growth and Change*, Supply and Services, Ottawa.

Economic Council of Canada (1976), *Efficiency and Regulation*, Supply and Services, Ottawa.

Economic Council of Canada (1977), *Living Together: A Study of Regional Disparities*, Supply and Services, Ottawa.

Economic Council of Canada (1982a), *Financing Confederation*, Supply and Services, Ottawa.

Economic Council of Canada (1982b), *Intervention and Efficiency*, Supply and Services, Ottawa.

Edel, *et al.* (1978), 'Uneven Regional Development: An Introduction to the Issue', *Review of Radical Political Economy*, Vol.10, Fall.

Finance Canada (1985), *The Regulation of Financial Institutions: Proposal for Discussion*, Queen's Printer, Ottawa.

Fischer, G.C. and Davis, R.H. (1976), 'The Impact of Multi-office Banking on the Availability of Credit in Smaller Communities', in *Compendium of Issues Relating to Branching by Federal Institutions*, U.S. Senate Committee on Banking, Housing and Urban Affairs, Subcommittee on Financial Institutions, Washington, D.C.

Fishkind, H.H. (1977), 'The Regional Impact of Monetary Policy: An Econometric Simulation Study of Indiana 1958-73', *Journal of Regional Science*, Vol.17, April.

Flechsig, T.G. (1965), 'The Effect of Concentration on Bank Loan Rates', *Journal of Finance*, Vol.20, May.

Fortin, P. (1982), 'Provincial Involvement in Regulating the Business Cycle: Justification, Scope and Terms', *Economic Council of Canada Discussion Paper*, Vol.213, February.

Frank, A.G. (1966), 'The Development of Underdevelopment', *Monthly Review*, September.

Frank, A.G. (1967), *Capitalism and Underdevelopment in Latin America*, Monthly Review Press, New York.

Frost, J.D. (1982), 'The "Nationalization" of the Bank of Nova Scotia, 1880-1910', *Acadiensis*, Vol.12, Autumn).

Fullerton, D (1979), 'Quebec Government Borrowing', Part I of Government of Canada (1979).

Garvy, G. (1959), *Debits and Clearing Statistics and Their Use*, Federal Reserve Board, Washington, D.C.

Gaskin, M. (1960), 'Credit Policy and the Regional Problem', *The Bankers' Magazine*, Vol.190, September.

Gaskin, M. (1965), *The Scottish Banks*, George Allen and Unwin, London.

Goldfeld, S.M. (1976), 'The Case of the Missing Money', *Brookings Papers on Economic Activity*, Vol.3.

168

Government of Canada (1973), *Capital Financing and Financial Institutions*, Western Economic Opportunities Conference, Calgary, July.

Government of Canada (1977),'Federal-Provincial Fiscal Arrangements and Established Programs Financing Act, *Finance Release*, 77-22, Ottawa (February 7).

Government of Canada (1978), *Sovereignty-Association - the Contradictions*, a report in the series Understanding Canada, Ottawa.

Government of Canada (1979), *Quebec: Access to Financial Markets*, a report in the series Understanding Canada, Ottawa.

Government of Canada (1980) *Proceedings of the Standing Senate Committee on National Finance*, Queen's Printer, Ottawa.

Government of Canada (1982) *Proceedings of the Standing Senate Committee on National Finance*, Queen's Printer, Ottawa.

Government of Canada (1984) *A New Direction for Canada: an Agenda for Economic Renewal*, report of the MacLaren Committee, Queen's Printer, Ottawa.

Government of Canada (1987), *The Canada-US Free Trade Agreement*, Queen's Printer, Ottawa.

Government of Manitoba (1973), *Guidelines for the Seventies*, Winnipeg, March.

Government of Manitoba (1982), *Budget Address*.

Government of Quebec (1969), *Report*, Study Committee on Financial Institutions (Parizeau), Quebec City.

Government of Quebec (1972), *Report*, Study Committee on the Securities Industry in Quebec (Bouchard), Quebec City.

Government of Quebec (1979), *Quebec-Canada: A New Deal*, Executive Council, Quebec City.

Government of Quebec (1980), *L'Epargne: Rapport du groupe de travail sur L'Epargne au Quebec*, Quebec City.

Guttentag, J.M. (1976), 'Branch Banking: A Summary of the Issues and the Evidence', in *Compendium of Issues Relating to Branching by Financial Institutions*, U.S. Senate Committee on Banking, Housing and Urban Affairs, Subcommittee on Financial Institutions, Washington, D.C., October.

Hammond, B. (1957), *Banks and Politics in America from the Revolution to the Civil War*, Princeton University Press, Princeton, reprinted in part in Easterbrook, W.T. and Watkins, M.H. (1967), *Approaches to Canadian Economic History*, McClelland and Stewart, Toronto.

Hewings, G.J.D. (1978), 'The Trade-off between Aggregate National Efficiency and Interregional Equity: Some Recent Empirical Evidence', *Economic Geography*, Vol.54, July.

Hicks, J.R. (1979), *Causality in Economics*, Basil Blackwell, Oxford.

Higgins, B. (1975), 'Trade-off Curves, Trends and Regional Disparities', *Economie Appliquee*, Vol, 28, No. 2-3.

Hogan, T.D. and Kaufman, H.M. (1977), 'Lags in Regional Adjustment to Changes in Monetary Policy,' *Quarterly Review of Economics and Business*, Vol.17, Winter.

Holland, S. (1976), *Capital versus the Regions*, St Martin's Press, New York.

Hood, W.C. (1958), *Financing of Economic Activity in Canada*, Royal Commission on Canada's Economic Prospects, Vol.18.

Howard, C.S. (1950), 'Canadian Banks and Bank Notes: A Record', *The Canadian Banker*, Vol.57, Winter.

Howe, C.D. Research Institute (1977), *Why Do the Balances Differ on Federal Receipts and Expenditures in Quebec?* C.D.Howe Research Institute, Montreal, September.

Ingram, J.C. (1959), 'State and Regional Payments Mechanisms', *Quarterly Journal of Economics*, Vol.73, November.

Jamieson, A.B. (1953), *Chartered Banking in Canada*, Ryerson, Toronto.

Jones, J.C.H. and Laudadio, L. (1972), 'Economies of Scale in Australian Banking: A Comment', *Economic Record*, Vol.48, December.

Kaldor, N. (1970), 'The Case for Regional Policies', *Scottish Journal of Political Economy*, Vol.17, November.

Kaliski, S.F. (1972), *The Trade-off Between Inflation and Unemployment: Some Explanations of the Recent Evidence for Canada*, Special Study No. 22, Economic Council of Canada, Ottawa.

Kerr, D.P. (1965), 'Some Aspects of the Geography of Finance in Canada', *The Canadian Geographer*, Vol.9 (4).

Keynes, J.M. (1936), *The General Theory of Employment, Interest and Money*, Macmillan, London.

Keynes, J.M. (1937), 'The General Theory of Employment', *Quarterly Journal of Economics*, Vol.51.

Kindleberger, C.P. (1974), 'The Formation of Financial Centres: A Study in Comparative Economic History', *Princeton Studies in International Finance* Vol.36.

Kregel, J. (1986), 'A Note on Finance, Liquidity, Saving and Investment', *Journal of Post Keynesian Economics*, Vol.9, Fall.

Lawson, T. (1989) 'Realism and Instrumentalism in the Development of Econometrics', *Oxford Economic Papers*, Vol. 41, January.

LaBrosse, J.R. (1980), 'Canada's Banking Legislation', *The Canadian Business Review*, Vol.7, Winter.

League for Social Reconstruction (1935), *Social Planning for Canada*, Nelson, Toronto.

Lenin, V.I. (1916, 1947) *Imperialism, The Highest Stage of Capitalism*, Foreign Languages Publishing House, Moscow.

Lipsey, R.G. (1960), 'The Relation Between Unemployment and the Rate of Change of Wage Rates in the UK, 1862-1957: A Further Analysis', *Economica* (New Series), Vol.27, February.

Lounsbury, F.E. (1960), *Financing Industrial Development in the Atlantic Provinces*, Atlantic Provinces Economic Council, Fredericton.

MacKay, R.A. (ed.) (1946), *Newfoundland: Economic, Diplomatic and Strategic Studies*, Oxford University Press, Toronto.

Mackintosh, W.A. (1935), *Economic Problems of the Prairie Provinces*, Macmillan, Toronto.

Mandel, E. (1973), *Capitalism and Regional Disparities*, New Hogtown Press, Toronto.

Mansell, R.L. and Copithorne, L. (1986), 'Canadian Regional Economic Disparities: A Survey', in Norrie, K.H. (ed.), *Disparities and Interregional Adjustment*, Research Study No. 64, University of Toronto Press, Toronto, for the Royal Commission on the Economic Union and Development Prospects for Canada, 1986.

Matthews, R. (1981), 'Two Alternative Explanations of the Problem of Regional Dependency in Canada', *Canadian Public Policy*, Vol.7, Spring.

Matthews, R. (1983), *The Creation of Rational Dependency*, University of Toronto Press, Toronto.

Maxwell, J. and Pestieau, C. (1980), *Economic Realities of Contemporary Confederation*, C.D. Howe Research Institute, Montreal.

McCall, A.S. (1980), 'The Impact of Bank Structure on Bank Service to Local Communities', *Journal of Bank Research*, Vol.11, Summer.

McCallum, J. (1980), *Unequal Beginnings: Agriculture and Development in Quebec and Ontario until 1870*, University of Toronto Press, Toronto.

McIvor, R.C. (1958), Canadian Monetary, Banking and Fiscal Development, *Macmillan, Toronto.*

McMillan, M.L. and Norrie, K.H. (1980), *'Province-Building versus a Rentier Society'*, Canadian Public Policy, *Vol.6, Supplement, February.*

Meyer, P.A. (1967), *'Price Discrimination, Regional Loan Rates and the Structure of the Banking Industry'*, Journal of Finance, *Vol.22, March.*

Miller, F.C. (1980), *'The Feasibility of Regionally Differentiated Fiscal Policies'*, Canadian Journal of Regional Science, *Vol.3, Spring.*

Miller, F.C. and Wallace, D.J. (1982), *'The Feasibility of Regionally Differentiated Fiscal Policies: Some Further Results'*, Canadian Journal of Regional Science.

Miller, R.J. (1978), The Regional Impact of Monetary Policy in the United States, *Lexington Books, Lexington, Mass.*

Mingo, J.T. (1975), *'Capital Management and Profitability of Prospective Holding Company Banks'*, Journal of Financial and Quantitative Analysis, *Vol.10, June.*

Minsky, H.P. (1975), John Maynard Keynes, *Macmillan, London.*

Mintz, J.M. (1979), *The Measure of Rates of Return in Canadian Banking*, Economic Council of Canada, Ottawa.

Moore, B.J. and Stuttman, S. (1984), 'A Causality Analysis of the Determinants of Money Growth', *British Review of Economic Issues*, Vol.6, Spring.

Moore, C.L. and Hill, J.M. (1982), 'Interregional Arbitrage and the Supply of Loanable Funds', *Journal of Regional Science*, Vol.22, November.

Mott, T. (1985-86), 'Towards a Post-Keynesian Formulation of Liquidity Preference', *Journal of Post Keynesian Economics*, 8 (Winter), 222-32.

Mundell, R.A. (1976), 'The International Distribution of Money in a Growing World Economy', in Frenkel, J.A. and Johnson, H.G. (eds.), *The Monetary Approach to the Balance of Payments*, University of Toronto Press, Toronto, 92-108.

Myatt, A. (1986), 'Money Supply Endogeneity: An Empirical Test for the United States, 1954-84', *Journal of Economic Issues*, 20 (March), 133-44.

Myrdal, G. (1964), *Economic Theory and Underdeveloped Regions*, Methuen, London.

Naylor, T. (1975), *The History of Canadian Business 1867-1914: The Banks and Finance Capital*, James Lorimer, Toronto.

Neufeld, E.P. (ed.) (1964), *Money and Banking in Canada*, McClelland and Stewart, Toronto.

Neufeld, E.P. (1972), *The Financial System of Canada*, St Martin's Press, New York.

Norrie, K.H. (ed.), *Disparities and Interregional Adjustment*, Research Study No. 64, University of Toronto Press, Toronto, for the Royal Commission on the Economic Union and Development Prospects for Canada.

Norrie, K.H. and Percy, M.B. (1981), 'Westward Shift and Interregional Adjustment: A Preliminary Report', *Economic Council of Canada Discussion Paper*, No. 201.

Ohlin, B.G. (1933), *Interregional and International Trade*. Harvard University Press, Cambridge, Mass.

173

Overton, J. (1978), 'Uneven Regional Development in Canada: The Case of Newfoundland', *Review of Radical Political Economy*, Vol.10, Fall.

Park, F.W. and L.C. (1973), *Anatomy of Big Business*, James Lewis and Samuel, Toronto.

Parker, C. (1978), 'What Price Quebec Independence', *The Banker*, Vol.128, June.

Passaris, C. (1975), 'Why Can't We Have a Regional Monetary Policy?' *Atlantic Advocate*, Vol.65, March.

Passaris, C. (1976), 'Finance Days: Finding a Cure for the Ailing Maritime Economy', *Atlantic Advocate*, Vol.66, February.

Passaris, C. (1977), 'Towards a Regional Monetary Policy in Canada', *Atlantic Economic Journal*, Vol.5, March.

Peters, D.D. (1976), 'The 1977 Bank Act: Comment', *Canadian Public Policy*, Vol.2, Summer.

Pfister, R.L. (1960), 'State and Regional Payments Mechanisms: Comment', *Quarterly Journal of Economics*, Vol.74, November.

Phillips, A. (1967), 'Evidence on Concentration in Banking Markets and Interest Rates', *Federal Reserve Bulletin*, June.

Phillips, P. (1978 and 1982), *Regional Disparities*, James Lorimer, Toronto.

Polese, M. (1981), 'Regional Disparity, Migration and Economic Adjustment: A Reappraisal', *Canadian Public Policy*, Vol.7, Autumn.

Premiers of Manitoba, Alberta, Saskatchewan and British Columbia (1973), *Capital Financing and Regional Financial Institutions*, Western Economic Opportunities Conference, Calgary, July.

Raynauld, A. (1980), 'La Bataille Des Comptes Economiques', *Textes Referendaires du Parti Liberal du Quebec*, Vol.4, January.

Richardson, D.R. (1986), 'Asimakopulos on Kalecki and Keynes on Finance, Investment and Saving', *Cambridge Journal of Economics*, Vol.10, June.

Rickover, R.M. (1976), 'The 1977 Bank Act: Emerging Issues and Policy Choices', *Canadian Public Policy*, Vol.2, Summer.

Robinson, J. (1952), 'The Rate of Interest', in *The Rate of Interest and Other Essays*, MacMillan, London.

Roy, N. (1986), *Mobility of Capital in the Canadian Economic Union*, Research Study No. 66, University of Toronto Press, Toronto, for the Royal Commission on the Economic Union and Development Prospects for Canada.

Royal Commission on Banking and Currency in Canada (Macmillan) (1933), *Report*, King's Printer, Ottawa.

Royal Commission on Banking and Finance (Porter) (1964), *Report*, Queen's Printer, Ottawa.

Royal Commission on Corporate Concentration (Bryce) (1978), *Report*, Queen's Printer, Ottawa.

Royal Commission on Dominion-Provincial Relations (Rowell-Sirois) (1940), *Report*, King's Printer, Ottawa.

Royal Commission on the Economic Union and Development Prospects for Canada (Macdonald) (1985), *Report*, Queen's Printer, Ottawa.

Ruffin, R.J. (1968), 'An Econometric Model of the Impact of Open Market Operations on Various Bank Classes', *Journal of Finance*, Vol.23, September.

Ryba, A. (1974a), 'Le Rôle du Secteur Financier dans le Developpement du Quebec: Un Essai en Finance Regionale', *Centre de Recherches en Developpement Economique, Universite de Montreal.*

Ryba, A. (1974b), 'Le Secteur Financier et le Developpement Economique du Quebec', *L'Actualite Economique*, Vol.50, July-September.

Ryba, A. (1976), 'L'Intermediation Financiere au Quebec: Les Institutions et les Marches', in Tremblay R. (ed.), *L'Economie Quebecoise: Histoire, Developpement, Politiques*, University of Quebec Press, Montreal.

Ryba, A. and Desnoyers, A. (1975), 'Le Secteur Financier et les Entreprises du Quebec', *Centre de Recherche en Developpement Economique, Universite de Montreal*, November.

Sacouman, R.J. (1981), 'The "Peripheral" Maritimes and Canada - Wide Marxist Political Economy', *Studies in Political Economy*, Vol.8, Autumn.

Samuelson, P.A. (1949), 'International Factor-Price Equalisation Once Again', *Economic Journal*, Vol.59, June.

Sarapkaya, S. (1978), 'Counting Canada's Banks', *The Canadian Banker*, Vol.85, December.

Savoie, D. (ed.) (1986), *The Canadian Economy: A Regional Perspective*, Methuen, Toronto.

Schultz, R. and Alexandroff, A. (1986), *Economic Regulation and the Federal System*, Research Study No. 42, University of Toronto Press, Toronto, for the Royal Commission on the Economic Union and Development Prospects for Canada.

Scitovsky, T. (1957), 'The Theory of the Balance of Payments and the Problem of a Common European Currency', *Kyklos*, Vol.10 (1).

Scott, I.O. (1955), 'The Regional Impact of Monetary Policy', *Quarterly Journal of Economics*, Vol.69, May.

Sears, J.T. (1972), *Institutional Financing of Small Business in Nova Scotia*, University of Toronto Press, Toronto.

Short, B.K. (1972), 'The Relation Between Commercial Bank Profit Rates and Banking Concentration in Canada, Western Europe and Japan', *Journal of Banking and Finance*, Vol.3, September.

Shortt, A. (1896), 'The Early History of Canadian Banking', *Journal of the Canadian Bankers' Association*, reprinted as 'Origin of the Canadian Banking System' in Neufeld (1964).

Sitwell, O.F.G. and Seifried, N.R.M. (1984), *The Regional Structure of the Canadian Economy*, Methuen, Toronto.

Snippe, J. (1985), 'Finance, Saving and Investment in Keynes's Economics', *Cambridge Journal of Economics*, Vol.9, September.

Straszheim, M.R. (1971), 'An Introduction and Overview of Regional Money Capital Markets', in Kain, J.F. and Meyer, J.R.(eds.), *Essays in Regional Economies*, Harvard University Press, Cambridge, Mass.

Sultan, R.G.M. (1977), 'Papers on the 1977 Bank Act Revision: A Comment', *Canadian Public Policy*, Vol.3, Winter.

Taylor, C.T. (1968), 'Average Interest Rates, the Loan Mix and Measures of Competition: Sixth Federal Reserve District Experience', *Journal of Finance*, Vol.23, December.

Thirlwall, A.P. (1980), 'Regional Problems are Balance-of-Payments Problems', *Regional Studies*, Vol.14 (5).

Thirlwall, A.P. (1986), 'A General Model of Growth Rate Development on Kaldorian Lines', *Oxford Economic Papers*, Vol.38, July.

Thirsk, W. (1973), *Regional Dimensions of Inflation and Unemployment*, Report for the Prices and Incomes Commission, Information Canada, Ottawa.

Thurston, T.B. (1976), 'Regional Interaction and the Reserve Adjustment Lag within the Commercial Banking Sector', *Journal of Finance*, Vol.31, December.

Tremblay, R. (1977), *Presentation des Comptes Economiques du Quebec, 1961-1975*, Editeur Official, Quebec City, 25 March.

Vanderkamp, J. (1986), 'The Efficiency of the Interregional Adjustment Process', in Norrie, 1986.

Veltmeyer, H.C. (1980), 'A Central Issue in Dependency Theory', *Canadian Review of Sociology and Anthropology*, Vol.17, August.

Walker, R.A. (1978), 'Two Sources of Uneven Development Under Advanced Capitalism: Spatial Differentiation and Capital Mobility', *Review of Radical Political Economy*, Vol.10, Fall.

Wallerstein, I. (1976), *The Modern World System*, Academic Press, New York.

Whalley, J. (1983), 'Induced Distortions of Inter-provincial Activity: An Overview of Issues', in Trebilcock, M.J., Prichard, J.R.S., Courchene, T.J., and Whalley, J. (eds.), *Federalism and Economic Union*, University of Toronto Press, Toronto, for the Ontario Economic Council.

Whitman, M. von N. (1967), 'International and Interregional Payments Adjustment: A Synthetic View', *Princeton Studies in International Finance*, Vol.19.

Whynes, D. (ed.) (1984), *What is Political Economy? Eight Perspectives*, Basil Blackwell, Oxford.

Williamson, J.G. (1965), 'Regional Inequalities and the Process of National Development', *Economic Development and Cultural Change*, Vol.13, July.

Wilson, T. (1968), 'The Regional Multiplier - A Critique', *Oxford Economic Papers*, Vol.20, November.

Wilson, T.A. (1977), 'The Province and Stabilization Policy', in OEC *Intergovernmental Relations: Issues and Alternatives* 1977, Ontario Economic Council, Toronto.

Wynant, L., Hatch J. and Grant, M.J. (1982), *Bank Financing of Small Business in Canada (Summary)*, University of Western Ontario, School of Business Admninistration, London, Ont.

Young, J.H. and Helliwell, J.F. (1964), 'The Effects of Monetary Policy on Corporations', in Royal Commission on Banking and Finance, *Appendix Volume*.

Author index

Subject index

184

187